ED'S
— ALL DAY
NUOUS HOURS
Mammoth
ATHON

ALL DAY

SAT., FEB. 21, 7 p.m.

STREET W.

Man-o-Man this is the Gal's Pyjam

A REAL MARATHON DANC

At 7 a.m. Wednesday morning, long before the doors o
who brave, strong toothsome couples will start dancing
and dancing with the hope that they will outlast each oth
be the ones to last right thru Honest Ed's Marathon Sale
thru the Charleston, the rumba, and
jiving throughout the night and the
table dancing the... winner was
by total of $1,000 in cash was the
lucky prize of

$1000

HOW TO BUILD AN EMPIRE ON AN ORANGE CRATE

OR 121 LESSONS I NEVER LEARNED IN SCHOOL

HONEST ED MIRVISH

HOW TO BUILD AN EMPIRE
ON AN ORANGE CRATE
OR
121 LESSONS I NEVER
LEARNED IN SCHOOL

KEY PORTER BOOKS

Canadian Cataloguing in Publication Data

Mirvish, Ed, 1914–
  How to build an empire on an orange crate

ISBN 1–55013–506–6

1. Mirvish, Ed, 1914–   —Quotations.
2. Success in business — Quotations, maxims, etc.
I. Title

HF5386.M5 1993   650.1′092   C93–094227–2

Key Porter Books Limited
70 The Esplanade
Toronto, Ontario
Canada M5E 1R2

The publisher gratefully acknowledges the assistance of the Canada
Council and Ontario Arts Council.

Frontispiece: My George Raft period!
Design: Scott Richardson
Typesetting: Ibex Graphic Communications Inc.
Printed and bound in Canada

93 94 95 96 97 6 5 4 3 2 1

CONTENTS

PREFACE

My name is Honest Ed.

Which alone is enough to make anyone suspicious.

If people think it's batty I don't blame them. After all, I chose the nickname myself. But then again, it never hurt Abe.

In fact, Mr. Lincoln and I have a few things in common. Both of us grew up poor. Neither of us had much schooling. He taught himself law; I taught myself business. We started from scratch and learned by experience. And each of us always bucked popular trends. Not that I'm comparing myself to Abraham. Hardly! I hate people who boast. But with "Honest" in front of your name you *must* tell the truth. And no matter how much I try, it's hard to be modest.

I began in business as a fifteen-year-old high school dropout with no money. I've never had a single partner or shareholder, except for my wife and son. I never went

HOW
TO
BUILD
AN
EMPIRE
ON AN
ORANGE
CRATE

public. Without shareholders, I never had to explain why I did outrageous things— nor why they misfired when they did. *I've only had to remember what went wrong, and not repeat it.*

People always tell me, "Ed, you have the Midas touch. Everything you touch turns to gold." Of course, nobody is always right, every time. But I learned long ago: *When it works, I tell the world. When it flops, I tell no one.*

This creates an amazing image of success.

When I got married, my bride, Anne, had an insurance policy with a cash surrender value of $212. With the money we started a tiny ladies' sportswear shop on our present Toronto location at Bloor and Bathurst. The rent was $55 a month.

A few years later we opened Honest Ed's on the same site, the first discount store, I'm told, in North America. On opening day we pulled in a hundred bucks. Today Honest Ed's is a Toronto tourist attraction. It grosses $65 million a year and covers an entire block. In one of the fifty-eight display windows surrounding it there's a sign which says: "Our Original Store Was Smaller Than This Window".

Behind Honest Ed's on Markham Street sits Mirvish Village— a name dedicated by the Mayor of Toronto. The village consists of twenty-three Victorian houses filled with bookstores, boutiques, small ethnic restaurants, crafts and antique shops, artists' studios, and art galleries. It was established as a place for individual artists and artisans to express themselves in creative ways— while

viii

leasing space at nominal rates. No *big* business is allowed in Mirvish Village.

To my constant astonishment, we now also own three world-class theatres. Two, of course, are internationally famous: the Royal Alexandra in Toronto, built in 1907, and the Old Vic in London, built in 1818. The third is the Princess of Wales in Toronto (just down the street from the Royal Alex) which we erected ourselves in 1993 — the first theatre to be privately constructed on this continent in more than ninety years. It was built especially to house our co-production of the super-hit *Miss Saigon*, the most expensive theatrical production ever mounted in Canada.

I still can't believe I'm in show biz. I'm basically a bargain merchant. I'd never had much interest in the arts, and bought the Royal Alex because I thought it was a *bargain*. For the next twenty years I went home and told my wife what a lousy business theatre was. Then one night I walked in and said, "Guess what, Anne? I just bought the Old Vic."

Between the two Toronto theatres on King Street, we also have a restaurant complex comprising Ed's Warehouse, Ed's Folly, Ed's Seafood, Ed's Italian, Old Ed's, and Most Honourable Ed's Chinese. Together they seat 2,600 diners. I never intended to be a restaurateur, either. But when I took over the Royal Alex, the neighbourhood was desolate. There were railway tracks across the street. So I bought the building next to the theatre and put in Ed's Warehouse — simply to give theatre-goers a pleasant

HOW
TO
BUILD
AN
EMPIRE
ON AN
ORANGE
CRATE

•
•
•
•
•
•
•
•
•
•
•
•
•
•
•
•
•
•
•
•
•
•
•
•
•
•
•
•
•
•
•
•
•
•
•
•

place to eat. The other restaurants weren't planned. Like most things I do, they just evolved. Sometimes I needed them just to store all the antiques we'd collected.

At any rate, I've gone from being a simple storekeeper to theatre and restaurant proprietor to producer through sheer ignorance. If I'd known at first what I was getting into, I probably wouldn't have. But that's in retrospect. The long shots paid off. And at least—with the store, theatres, and dining rooms combined—I'm able to pay the salaries of 1,400 employees.

Over the years, in recognition of my often misguided efforts, I've been privileged to have received nearly two hundred awards and honorary degrees. Besides the Order of Canada, I was truly humbled (which is rare) to have received from Queen Elizabeth the CBE—Commander of the Order of the British Empire. It made me the first Canadian living outside of England to receive this honour in twenty-five years.

Not bad for a former fifteen-year-old dropout. It makes me wonder if I shouldn't have left school *sooner*.

Still, as pleased as I was to receive a Harvard Chair from the Harvard School of Business, the declaration naming me a Freeman of the City of London was perhaps more apropros. It gives me the right to herd sheep across London Bridge without paying a toll. But far more significantly, while I can still be executed for a crime, they *have* to hang me with a silken, not a hemp rope.

Now, *that's* something to look forward to. My old pals say it's long overdue. When they ask me what my CBE means, I tell them it stands for "Creator of Bargains Everywhere".

For that's what I am. Honest Ed, the bargain man. I'll tell you how it all began.

•
•
•
•
•
•
•
•
•
•
•
•
•
•
•
•
•
•
•
•
•
•
•
•
•
•
•
•
•
•
•
•
•
•
•
•
•
•
•
•
•
•
•
•
•
•

CHAPTER ONE

Many of the kids I grew up with in downtown Toronto wound up either dead or in prison.

It was a tough Jewish neighbourhood abounding with bookies, bootleggers, and immigrant shopkeepers. The kids had three choices: go to work, go to school, or go to jail.

I managed to avoid the last choice because my parents insisted I go to school. And also, ever since I was nine, I worked because I *had* to. My dad and mom ran a small grocery store on Dundas Street West, open from 7 A.M. till 2 the next morning. My mother, Anna, toiled hard all her life. My father, David, was a dreamer. He loved to sit in the store and read up to six newspapers a day. He also gave credit to customers who couldn't pay. Which is why the store was always insolvent—and why, after school, I worked.

It's not that my dad was averse to success. He'd tried

HOW
TO
BUILD
AN
EMPIRE
ON AN
ORANGE
CRATE

to make it at different times. But success always seemed to shun *him*. Educated to be a rabbi in Russia, he wound up selling Masonic encylopedias in America. His own father was a notary public in Kiev who, while notarizing a last will, caught his client's typhoid fever and died four months before his son was born.

My grandmother Mirvish never left Kiev. But before the pogroms started, she sent her three children to America. David, my father, was the last to leave. After six lonely weeks in steerage, he arrived in Baltimore. He was thirteen. But once he arrived, he was no longer alone — or in desperate need of money. One of his sisters, Jennie, had married a man named Louis Herman who soon became the city's biggest wholesale auctioneer. The eldest sister, Rebecca, had wed Harry Mensh, an entrepreneur who was even richer.

Rebecca and Harry Mensh lived in Colonial Beach, Virginia. Six hours by excursion boat up the Potomac from Washington, D.C., it was a thriving, sun-drenched summer spa luring families from New York and Pennsylvania. But it might as well have been called "Mensh Beach", since most of it was Harry's.

He owned the raucous shooting galleries, gaming concessions, and kiosks on the bustling boardwalk by the beach, and fertile orchard groves at each end. He owned the elegant Crown Castle Hotel (for Jewish clientele) and another swank inn for gentiles. He owned two restaurants, a movie house, an outdoor cinema, and a dance pavilion on a pier. Harry also owned the Workingmen's

Exchange, a combination tavern, pool hall, and supply store for crab and oyster fishermen.

With his handlebar moustache, long slim cigars, white linen suits, and mint juleps, Harry loved to pose as a grand Virginia gentleman, and often alluded to the slaves on his plantation—although the only obvious black man in his employ was an ancient character named Boodie who drove a wagon down the boardwalk daily, advertising the current features in Harry's cinemas.

My father loved the sun and excitement of Colonial Beach when he visited his sister: the crowds on the boardwalk, the big white yachts festooned with flags, the music on the dance pier, and the hustle of the hotel. He wanted to stay there. But Harry Mensh had a brother, Sam, who owned a saloon in Baltimore. Mensh's Buffet, it was called. And that's where my dad first went to work.

He wore a white apron that hung to his shins and swept the floor, spread sawdust, rinsed beer mugs, stacked cases of Brightwood Club Whiskey, and pulled the beer pumps. I have a photograph of my father standing in front of Mensh's Buffet with five other men. He is small, with a timid smile, and holds a cigarette between two fingers. Even then, he chain-smoked. Also in the picture is the imposing Harry Mensh, with both his shoulders and his moustache stiff.

Another teenaged clerk in Mensh's Buffet was an Austrian, Jake Kornhauser. Jake had a younger sister named Anna who at thirteen, like my father David, had sailed

HOW
TO
BUILD
AN
EMPIRE
ON AN
ORANGE
CRATE

alone in steerage to America. They'd arrived in Baltimore the same year. Anna lived with her brother Jake, working by day and studying English at night school. She was beautiful. When my dad and Jake moved to Colonial Beach as barmen in the Workingmen's Exchange, Anna joined them.

The three teenage immigrants became close friends. And David and Anna fell in love. But in 1909, when my dad was nineteen, he met a slick-tongued salesman named Charlie Bolts who travelled the States, peddling copies of *The Encyclopedia of Freemasonry*. Bolts was looking for a young assistant. So, lured by the promise of instant riches, my father trekked with Charlie into America's vast Bible Belt where small-town citizens shelled out forty-two bucks for a set of volumes revealing dark Vatican plots and Masonic mysteries.

Charlie Bolts made the pitches. My dad packaged and collected. As Bolts had promised, they pulled in piles of money — most of which Charlie pocketed. My father got the experience.

But even after that, his initial stab into business, he never became hard-nosed nor cynical. He went back to his job in the Workingmen's Exchange. And when both he and Anna were twenty-two, they married. The newly-weds moved into an apartment over the dry-goods store owned by Emmanuel Fox (who'd married one of the Mensh girls). Then two years later, the Panama Canal opened, World War I began, and the Mirvishes had a son.

This, I'm delighted to say, is where I come in. On July 24, 1914, in fact. I beat the war by four days.

To perform the initial rites of birth, a rabbi named Yoelson was imported from Washington since there wasn't one in Colonial Beach. At the party afterwards, Rabbi Yoelson, I'm told, went on about his wayward son who'd rejected the rabbinate to appear on Broadway. Thirteen years later the rabbi's son starred in the first talking picture, *The Jazz Singer*. I always say my chief claim to fame was being circumcised by Al Jolson's dad.

My parents named me Yehuda. Fortunately, I had a worldly older cousin, Frances, who instantly Americanized the name to Edwin. Thank goodness for Frances. I've heard enough snickers over my name as it is. Just imagine if I'd opened a store named "Honest Yehuda's".

Frances was a special lady — smart, beautiful, glamorous. She raced horses, pitched horseshoes, figure skated, and wore scarlet capes in Washington. One of my aunt Rebecca Mensh's eight children, Frances became wealthy, adored, and wonderfully old without ever marrying. Men, including boys like me, automatically loved her. She was the Lillie Langtree of the early 1900s.

While working with a Washington patent attorney, she met one of his clients, Irving Berlin. Then for years, as Irving's "private secretary", she circled the globe with the celebrated songwriter. She later repeated the role with the renowned but eccentric inventor Laurens Hammond, best remembered for inventing the Hammond organ, who lived in a castle in Gloucester, Mass., with a private

HOW
TO
BUILD
AN
EMPIRE
ON AN
ORANGE
CRATE

cemetery in which to bury his cats while they waited for reincarnation. Like Spencer Tracy, Hammond was rich, Roman Catholic, and unable to divorce his wife. But he gave Frances (who adored felines too) a huge Manhattan brownstone mansion with elevators where she lived out her years as a truly grand grande dame with a cross-eyed Siamese cat named Prince Chichibu.

I still remember Frances taking me, as a toddler, on the sunny, six-hour excursion trips up the Potomac from Washington, D.C., as a band played on the deck. We'd moved to the capital when I was two because my father decided to start his own grocery business. Mainly, he wanted out from under the thumb of his brother-in-law Harry Mensh and to be his own boss. Also my uncle, Jake Kornhauser, was already in Washington running his own small grocery, and my parents wanted to be near him.

So they rented a store on the corner of T Street and New Hampshire Avenue, which seemed like a smart move at first. My dad loved talking to customers, and my mother liked to work. Not long afterward, when Prohibition hit America, bartenders at the Workingmen's Exchange were out of work anyway.

As for me, growing up in Washington was wonderful. My dad would take me to B. F. Keith's famous vaudeville theatre and (in deference to his religious training in Kiev) to all high holidays at the synagogue. Every Easter, I'd troop off with my horde of cousins and hunt coloured eggs on the White House lawn. Then after school (at Adam's P.S.) we'd often race off to Uncle Jack's store in one of the city's black enclaves. From his rooftop we could look right into the baseball park and see Ty Cobb and Babe Ruth slug it out with the Senators. But the free ball games ended when Uncle Jack got shot.

One night a riot broke out in his neighbourhood and the militia were ordered in. Jake's black customers begged him to close his store; they'd heard that two other black men planned to rob him. But Jake stayed open. And, during the rioting, two men walked in and shot him. A gentle Orthodox Jew who prayed every day, Jake never could understand it. After he recovered, my uncle sold his grocery and opened a variety store near us. After that, we had to pay to see the Senators.

Circuses and Saturday matinees were also big attractions. My first entrepreneurial venture, in fact, was cashing in on the movie craze. I pasted a whole bunch of comic strips together, then slowly pulled them through one end of a shoebox while my customers peered through an opposite hole. I charged one cent per peep. But I never became D.W. Griffith. Or rich. (Still, now that I'm producing shows, it's ironic to think I started in show biz at eight. I should have learned from the experience.)

The only one of my childhood chums who became famous at the time was my cousin Stanley Mensh. Stanley peddled newspapers on a street corner near the White House. One evening during a downpour a black limousine stopped at his corner, and the man in the back seat waved Stanley in from the rain. A passing

HOW
TO
BUILD
AN
EMPIRE
ON AN
ORANGE
CRATE

photographer snapped the picture. And the next day, on the front page of the Washington papers, there sat my soaking cousin Stanley in the limo beside Woodrow Wilson. For once, the president was actually smiling.

As a child I spent every summer in Colonial Beach. Frances would take me up the river, and I'd stay in Aunt Rebecca's big house with my cousins. Of the eight of them, some, like Frances, were already working. Marcus became a big Washington florist who decorated all the embassies. And Dave made movies in California. But the youngest, like Benny, were still at home.

Benny was two years older than me, and my hero. He and Frances would take me crab fishing in Chesapeake Bay in one of their father's rental boats. They'd teach me to pull the line up so slowly the crab didn't even know he was moving—then swiftly scoop the little rascal in a net. We'd sail, we'd swim, we'd have picnics on the beach. When new movies came in, we'd go see them.

One night I crawled under my seat in the outdoor theatre and fell asleep. Benny was so absorbed in the picture, he didn't notice. When the movie ended, I wasn't there. There was instant pandemonium in Colonial Beach. Harry Mensh himself led the posse. Finally, after two hours of hollering my name through megaphones, someone in the search party found me. I woke up and asked where the movie was.

At the back of the Crown Castle Hotel was a large, screened-in dining lounge looking out over gardens and a sweeping lawn. Benny and I pitched a tent out there and, while listening to the murmur of the diners, we'd fall asleep and spend the nights.

Every morning we'd dash to the Workingmen's Exchange where Uncle Harry would mix us a milk punch. To a shaker of milk he added one scoop of sugar, one raw egg, and one shot of whiskey. Thus the "punch". I drank more as a kid than I ever have since. I decided at nine that I'd better taper off. At nine, I also quit smoking. I took one puff of a cigarette, got sick as a mongrel, and have never touched one since. Sometimes I learn fast. When I say I've stopped smoking, and people ask when, I tell them, "The year Jack Dempsey knocked out Firpo."

Those were my two childhood vices; I've avoided all others since. But I must admit in fairness, Harry's milk punches *did* start off the day with a glow.

After drinking breakfast, Benny and I usually raced down the boardwalk to find Boodie's horse and wagon. We'd jump up behind him and squat beneath the movie posters as he clomped along clanging a brass handbell. Boodie was conscientious, but also adventurous. Often he'd come to the end of the boardwalk—and keep right on going. Out through the orchard groves into the countryside.

Soon we'd be a couple of miles from town. Not a building, soul or dog in sight. But good old Boodie kept on jangling that bell and croaking out the news that Mister Cee Bee Dee-Mille was currently presenting *The Ten Commandments*, or Douglas Fairbanks was coming next as the *Thief of Bagdad*. Even when he rode *alone* into the

HOW
TO
BUILD
AN
EMPIRE
ON AN
ORANGE
CRATE

country, Boodie continued his announcements. We thought it was hilarious.

Before I met him, the only blacks I'd paid much attention to were the contestants in Colonial Beach's popular watermelon-eating contests. They'd gobble down as many melons as they could, bob their faces into flour barrels, then come up grinning. Instant whiteface. The surrounding spectators from Philly, Bayonne, and Newark howled. But Boodie, I noticed, never laughed.

He and my cousin Benny became two close buddies, and both are long gone. Boodie of arrested longevity, and Benny—no one knows. He became a reporter for a Washington D.C. paper, and was sent to cover a story in Cuba. He arrived in Havana. Then disappeared. No one ever saw him again. I miss them both.

One other old black man I also miss was a former slave named Uncle Steve, who worked for my parents in their Washington grocery. Already in his seventies by then, he remembered being pulled from his parents' arms as a lad and sold to a different owner. Perhaps because of his own sad childhood, he became my great protector. When I was unruly, my dad would lock me in a shed behind the store. Uncle Steve always let me out. He'd go to my father and waggle his finger. "Oh Mister Mirvish, you mustn't *do* that. Eddie's just a little boy." I adored Uncle Steve.

His main job was plucking chickens in the shed, and I'd watch him toss them in vats of steaming water before yanking out the feathers. My mother kept the feathers and stuffed them in flour sacks to be used as pillows. The sugar bags she saved to make into underwear. As a kid all my underwear had huge red Xs on it.

Meanwhile, due mainly to my dad's business savvy, the grocery store was steadily sinking in debt. What's more, there was also another mouth to feed when my brother Robert, whom Frances also named, was born in 1921. My dad's only assets were shares he'd bought in a Florida land company. Yet one of the Menshs had checked the site and reported it was perfect for anyone enamoured with wall-to-wall swamp. I still have those shares in a bottom drawer. Who knows? I may be a thriving alligator owner.

By 1923, my parents' store had hit dead bottom when who should suddenly show up again but that slick old Mason maven, Charlie Bolts. Though no one was exactly overjoyed to see him, I must admit in retrospect that his arrival changed my life.

My dad told Bolts how depressed he was about Jake's shooting, supporting his sons, the Florida swamp, and looming bankruptcy. But Charlie seemed delighted. "Thank God," he said, beaming. "You're just the man I'm looking for. The timing's perfect."

My father had heard the exact line before, but once again he bit, "For what?"

"You're forgetting your *greatest* asset, my boy," crooned Charlie. "You're a *Mason*!"

And indeed my father was. He and Harry Mensh, in

HOW
TO
BUILD
AN
EMPIRE
ON AN
ORANGE
CRATE

fact, were the only Jewish Masons in the Colonial Beach Lodge. And my father had risen through the ranks to become a *thirty-second-degree* Mason, at that. He had served the order faithfully, Charlie intoned, and the order would now provide *his* salvation.

"You mean," said my dad, "you want me to go back out selling books through the States?"

"*No*, David, *NO*," thundered Charlie. "In a brand *new* territory. *Canada!*"

And that's how the Mirvishes became Canadians.

The Encyclopedia of Freemasonry, Bolts explained, had never sold well north of the border. A regrettable fact—but *not* irreversible. So to meet the challenge, an outfit named Virtue & Co. Limited was opening an office to sell the encyclopedias on Church Street in Toronto. And my dad, Charlie assured him, was the ideal man for the job. "Just *think*," he enthused, "of the *opportunity*."

Well, in short, there were no opportunities left in Washington. So my dad accepted. Perhaps he should have gone to Toronto alone at first to check it out. But he refused to leave his family. The last time he'd travelled to a new country, he'd been alone, and lonely. He wouldn't do it again.

And so we all went north together in the spring of 1923. I was nine, and in grade four. All the Menshs and Kornhausers and cousins came to say good-bye. Uncle Steve wept when we left.

CHAPTER TWO

In 1923 Hitler staged his Beer Hall Putsch in Munich,
Pancho Villa was shot in Mexico, earthquakes killed
120,000 in Japan, Douglas Fairbanks became Robin
Hood, and my dad arrived to conquer Canada.

He rented a house at 89 St. Clarens Avenue in downtown Toronto, then set out by streetcar to barnstorm the
city. The trips between Masonic Temples were short.
There were dozens of lodges in town, and thousands of
Masons. The Masons *ran* Toronto. If a member sometimes bent the law, he rarely went to prison; all the cops,
lawyers, judges, and jailers were Masons. Toronto the
Good was a *big* Masonic city.

My dad was elated. (Charlie Bolts, for once, had been
right! Opportunity abounded.) He tore around to the
Masonic Temples and delivered the same spiel Bolts had
pitched in the south. He gave lectures. He collared cops

HOW
TO
BUILD
AN
EMPIRE
ON AN
ORANGE
CRATE

in station houses and repeated the patter. And his fellow Masons were fascinated.

There was only one hitch. None of them wanted to shell out fifty dollars for a set of encyclopedias. In the days when a corned beef sandwich cost a nickle, fifty bucks was a fortune. It took my father a while to catch on. By then he was exhausted—the rheumatic fever he'd had as a child kept him weak all his life—and still without means. So one morning he woke up and quit the encyclopedia business.

We moved to a much cheaper house at 241 Markham Street—just south of the present Mirvish Village—where my dad (he never learned) signed on as a Fuller Brush man. But a Fuller suitcase was even heavier than a set of books—and sales less lucrative still. So reluctantly, he quit again. My mother didn't argue. Slick salesmanship, she agreed, was obviously not his forte.

What we existed on during those first two years in Toronto, I don't know. Besides, with my sister Lorraine's birth in 1923, there were three kids by then. Finally in 1925 my parents moved again to a store at 788 Dundas Street. They'd decided that groceries were the only thing they knew how to sell—no matter how disastrously. "People *have* to eat," my father said, forgetting the fact it wasn't necessarily *our* groceries they'd want. But still, Toronto wasn't Washington. Perhaps a new city offered hope.

And so, for the second time, "D. Mirvish Groceries" opened for business. But business was hardly brisk. After paying bills and feeding the family, my parents didn't make enough to restock what they sold. So they started renting rooms to tenants. And my dad took a second job as a "candy butcher" on the railroad. Every few days, leaving my mom to run the store, he'd ride a train to Winnipeg and back—selling candy bars, magazines, sandwiches, and sodas to the coach passengers.

For the first time as a salesman he had captive customers, and with tips and commission, he was soon making money. My mother was thrilled. But after seven months or so, the day and night trips down the aisles got exhausting, and he missed his family. So he quit his third selling job in Toronto to stay in the store, which he never left till he died.

There were floor-to-ceiling shelves bearing cans, bags, and boxes on all three inside walls, and a counter along the right side. The counter edge was tattooed with the burns of my father's cigarettes (nearly three packs of Honeysuckles daily, at ten cents a pack), which he'd often set down and forget. A huge iron weigh-scale loomed atop the counter, and beside it in the icebox sat a tub of butter (sold by the scoop) and a huge can of sour cream (sold by the cup). Since the neighbourhood women shopped for the day's bagels and butter before breakfast, the store opened promptly at 7 A.M. —and rarely closed before 2 in the morning.

Through a door at the back of the store was the "sitting room" where my parents also slept with my baby sister. Behind it was the tiny kitchen where my mother cooked, and a bathroom beside it. Stairs at the back led

HOW
TO
BUILD
AN
EMPIRE
ON AN
ORANGE
CRATE

to three rooms upstairs. The front and back rooms were rented to tenants, while Bob and I shared the room in between.

Over the years, tenants came and went. One was a big, blond kid named Ben who lived upstairs with his parents. Every summer morning Ben got up before dawn to swim for hours in Lake Ontario. Later he became a famous long-distance swimmer. Ben's dad was a drunken ex-cop who'd been kicked off the force. When Ben was swimming and his mother off working in a laundry, the father would often sell their furniture to buy booze. Ben would then beat his dad up and his mom would call the cops—who would never book their old buddy.

Not all the tenants were as lucky. One was a flasher who'd ride the streetcar to Eaton's department store on Saturday afternoons for the sole purpose of dropping his pants in front of women. He finally left us when he moved to jail. Much to the relief of both my mother and Eaton's.

There was also a big black man named Rigg who lived upstairs with a blonde girl. One night Rigg returned from the racetrack with Larry Gains, a black British heavyweight boxer, and another blonde. In the middle of the night, Bob and I were suddenly awakened by the two screaming women. Rigg and Gains were smashing each other into the walls. It took the cops (who knew us well by then) to break it up. Rigg was bloody but still standing. He was lucky. A few years later his pal Larry Gains won decisions over two world heavyweight champions,

Max Schmeling and Primo Carnera, and became the British Empire heavyweight champ himself.

The tenant who stayed the longest was tiny Rabbi Dinkin. For nearly five years he slept in the back room and conducted a Hebrew school in the front one. Every day about fifty students showed up for separate classes running two hours each, while Rabbi Dinkin tossed his ruler at them.

There was always bedlam in those upstairs rooms. But the noise was a minor nuisance, compared with the bathroom. Just think about it: five Mirvishes, Rabbi Dinkin, fifty students, and *one* toilet.

I haven't even added the customers who asked to use it. My dad often kept them talking so long in the store that they *had* to. When my father wasn't talking, smoking, burning his counter, or giving credit, he read. Besides his library of Freemason books, he devoured Jules Verne and Sholem Aleichem. And besides the three daily newspapers and *Hebrew Journal* published in Toronto, he bought both the New York *Daily Mirror* and *Jewish Forward*.

He also took correspondence courses in bookkeeping. Not that they did any good. Most of the entries were for credit.

Every morning my father walked up Dundas for a ten-cent shave in Halperin's Barber Shop. Halperin kept my dad's private shaving mug and razor on his shelf. When my dad didn't have a dime, Halperin took payment in groceries.

HOW
TO
BUILD
AN
EMPIRE
ON AN
ORANGE
CRATE

My father also loved five-cent shoeshines, cuff links, studs, and the gold watch chain stretched across his vest. When business was *really* bad, the accessories sat in a pawnbroker's window. Sometimes he'd go fishing in Lake Ontario, or place a racing bet with a bookie. Bookies, bootleggers, and petty thieves were the store's best customers. They all paid cash.

And the neighbourhood was rife with them. The bootleggers used straight alcohol in their concoctions. When customers dropped in, they'd get a free glass of cherry brandy. One gulp would straighten a paper clip. One day the cops raided a convention of booze-vendors down the street. "We're not bootleggers," one of them shouted. "We're *house-painters*." After that, to the moonshiners' mortification, grinning clients would order twenty-sixers of rum-based "enamel".

There were Ukrainians, Hungarians, Poles, and Italians in the area, but the vast majority were Jewish immigrants who'd fled every country in Europe. All the merchants on Dundas Street were Jews. There was Freeman's shoe store, Kalb's Delicatessen, Brightman's grocery, Tractor's Creamery, two fruit stores, Rosenberg's and Shimkofsky's, and two butcher shops, Max Wall's and Max Goldman's—which was next door to ours.

There was also Doc Pearlman's office down the street, which was packed all day with dozens of patients. Then at night he'd go out at any hour on emergencies. Like my father, he gave almost everyone credit. His job, he felt, was to service the sick, not profit by them. When the

Depression hit, and the poor became poorer, he scooped up all the unpaid bills from his desk one night and burned them in his furnace. Doc Pearlman, like the rabbi around the corner, was revered in our neighbourhood.

The kids I grew up with had names like Swinky, Maxie, and Mushmellow. Some (unlike Swinky) managed to stay out of jail; a few even suceeded in *becoming* somebody. Like Leon Weinstein, who became president of Loblaw's grocery chain. And Brightman the grocer's son who became a dentist—and operated on Winston Churchill during the war when he met with Roosevelt in Quebec. And Lou Jacobi who became an actor ("Moustache" in *Irma La Douce*), Baby Yack the boxer, and referee-boxer Sammy Luftspring.

Ben Haberman never became famous, but I'll not forget him. Ben was my very first partner in crime. I was eleven. Some Italian kids had been showing us all the stuff they'd stolen from the Canadian National Exhibition on the waterfront, the world's biggest annual fair. *Great* stuff—toy pandas, model planes, baseball caps— stuff Ben and I had never had. So the next afternoon we hit the CNE ourselves.

We got through the ticket gates by lying. Choking back sobs, we said we'd left the grounds by accident— and our parents were still *inside*. Who could resist a line like that? *In* we went. We charged directly to the souvenir stands on the midway where Ben stood beside the counters, and I stood a few feet back as the lookout. When the vendor turned his head away, I'd wave at Ben.

HOW
TO
BUILD
AN
EMPIRE
ON AN
ORANGE
CRATE

And Ben would swiftly scoop all the prizes he could into a shopping bag. Then we'd both bolt into the crowd. We hit half a dozen stalls that way, and by dark had filled two bags.

Our crime spree had been a roaring success. The trouble came when we got home. I went first to Ben's place to stash our loot—and his parents and big brother were waiting. It was after 11 P.M. *Where* had we been? At the Ex, we said, and they checked our bulging bags. Shrieks from Ben's mom when she saw the booty. We *won* it all, Ben protested.

Ben's brother was a lawyer. "You two played the games?" he asked. Ben nodded. "And *what*," he thundered, "did you use for *money*?"

That did it. Justice was swift. Ben's brother simply grabbed both the bags and fired them into the kitchen coal stove. I've never gotten over that. It was one thing to burn Ben's bag. After all, he was his brother. But why *mine*?

When my mild-mannered father heard his son was a criminal, even he erupted. Ben Haberman and I were forbidden to see each other for a month.

And then there was Yale Simpson—who the downstairs lounge in the Royal Alexandra Theatre is named after. Yale and I became lifelong friends.

His father had been a tenant farmer on 100-acres abutting Yonge Street in North Toronto. When the farmland (now worth millions) was put up for sale, Yale's dad couldn't raise the $7,000. So he moved his family down to Markham Street, which *our* family had previously lived on, and kept horses in a stable behind the house. He'd buy a string in the countryside, lead them home in a caravan behind the horse he rode, then sell them to milk, bread, and ice companies to haul their deliveries.

But I didn't meet Yale until his family opened a fruit store on Dundas, when both of us were twelve. In those days just prior to the Depression, there weren't many things for poor kids to do. In our neighbourhood they either played in parks with a local ball team, such as the Maccabees, Judeans, or Gorevale Avenue Rats, or battled in back alleys with the Markham Street Gang (Jewish) or Mansfield Avenue Gang (Italian). Since neither Yale nor I was much interested in sports, black eyes, or girls at the time, we invented our own activities.

We scampered around to junk shops and scrounged spare radio parts to build a crystal set with two sets of earphones. Then we'd huddle around it for hours listening to all the big dance bands, Amos 'n' Andy, the latest hit songs ("Bye, Bye, Blackbird" and "The Desert Song") and news of Gertrude Ederle swimming the English Channel or Babe Ruth slugging in sixty homers.

Then one day we found a whole bunch of toasters in a scrap pile. Yale pulled out all the filaments, connected them together, and twisted them into shapes spelling out our names. Then we stuck them onto sheets of asbestos on my bedroom wall. And . . . Presto! When we plugged it in, there were our names, glowing like neon lights. There

HOW
TO
BUILD
AN
EMPIRE
ON AN
ORANGE
CRATE

was just one hitch: it also blew all the fuses in the store. My dad, reading his papers downstairs, was suddenly plunged into darkness. Our signs had an instant demise.

But instead of throwing the elements out, we connected them to a tin plate in the kitchen. Then we'd grab a stray cat in the alley behind. (There were dozens in the neighbourhood because of all the rats.) We'd bring in the cat, fill the plate with milk, and let the kitty at it. Forget that Russian dog in *Sputnik*. When our cats lapped that milk they'd go into instant orbit—their tails sticking straight in the air.

My dad couldn't figure out what all the unholy shrieks were about. By the time he hit the kitchen, of course, the cats would be streaking through Alberta. The only alien object was an innocent saucer of milk. But when he *did* find out, Yale and I wished that we'd gone west too.

A few times, though, we escaped detection. The day Max Goldman's son got married next door, we called Deer Park Limousine and ordered six cars and chauffeurs for the wedding party. Then we watched from our roof as the limos pulled up. The ensuing bedlam was better than any Fairbanks flick. Max yanked the cleaver from his butcher's block and swore he'd split the culprit's skull when he found out who he was. Fortunately, he never did.

We also hung around with a kid named Sam Sniderman (*not* the future "Record Man"), whose dad had a tailor shop on Harbord Street. He was older than us, about eighteen, and was wild about all racing machines like planes and motorcycles. Sniderman already owned a motorcycle, but no plane. So one summer he rounded up about twelve of us to form the Dundas Street Glider Club. What he really wanted was slave labour, for the club's sole purpose was to build a glider, then fly it.

But build one, we did. With wire, canvas, glue, and orange crates, a splendid single-seater. Each member was promised a chance to fly it solo. But early one Saturday morning, Sniderman and another guy sneaked the glider out to High Park, and attached it to a towline behind the motorcycle. The other guy drove the cycle; Sniderman was the pilot. The bike roared off across the park. The glider soared up behind it and hit a tree. Sniderman broke his leg. Even worse, the glider was smashed into smithereens.

The members were furious at Sniderman's treachery and the fact they never had a chance to fly, but delighted to learn of the divine retribution. It was, however, the instant death of the glider club.

But Sniderman's bike and plane still intrigued us. Yale and I bought an old twin-cylinder Indian motorcycle for five bucks, and the front-end frame and steering wheel of a Model T Ford. Then we made this weird, triangular three-wheel vehicle by attaching the back of the cycle to the front of the Ford. Finally, we carved a big propeller from birch wood and mounted it onto the motorcycle engine in front. Yale was a whiz at this stuff. Then we'd spin the prop, snap on the ignition, and—believe it or

HOW
TO
BUILD
AN
EMPIRE
ON AN
ORANGE
CRATE

not—that contraption tore down the alley behind our
store at eighteen miles an hour.

For one entire summer we roared up and down that
alley, shooting flames from the exhaust. To the neighbourhood kids, Yale and I were the Wright brothers. We
were famous. Until the day some delivery man who must
have been stone deaf opened a garage door into the alley
just as we approached. The door was instantly shattered
into toothpicks. The *Kitty Hawk* of Dundas Street looked
like a modern sculpture. And the Wright brothers' fame
abruptly ended—not with a whimper but a bang.

One autumn morning in 1927, Yale and I started off
along Dundas for our first day of high school. I was supposed to go to Central School of Commerce, and Yale to
Harbord Collegiate. But neither of us wanted to split up.
So we went instead to Central Technical School where,
without even a raised eyebrow, they accepted us both in
the industrial class. Even more amazing, our parents
didn't seem to mind—as long as we went to school. Yale
stayed five years, switched to the academic course, and
graduated. I stayed two years. I wasn't a terrific student,
but I always passed my exams.

We joined no sports or extra-curricular activities—
not by choice, but because we had no time. Immediately
after classes each day, we both hurried home to work in
our stores. I knew my mom needed help. From dawn till
late in the night she served customers, cleaned clothes,
sifted ashes, scrubbed floors, cooked meals, and baked
bread in our Happy Thought stove, which she shined

with Nonsuch Stove Polish to keep black. She hardly ever left the store. Never once, for instance, in the fourteen years she was there, did she ever step inside the Duchess Theatre down the street. She worked every day of her life.

So I helped all I could. My chores were to carry crates and boxes from the basement, stack shelves, and keep the fruit bins filled out front. But my main job was delivering. Each day at four I'd bicycle around the neighbourhood for an hour, taking orders. I *had* to, because we didn't have a phone. Riding back to the store I'd fill out the orders, then go out again to deliver them. On Sunday afternoons, I'd tour all the houses again to collect. *That* was the hard part. If they had no money, and most of them didn't, they just wouldn't answer my knock. I spent a lot of time on doorsteps.

By far the happiest time in my week was Sunday morning, between 2 A.M. and dawn. I'd go with Harold Gibbon, who worked for Max Wall the butcher, on his rounds. After closing our shop, I'd climb into his truck, and we'd ride a couple of miles up Bathurst to Forest Hill, a lush, elm-shaded enclave of huge stone houses. It was here where most of Max's wealthier Jewish customers lived, and all night I'd help him carry the meat up silent driveways to back doors and deposit it in their milk boxes. Then, just before sunrise we'd head back downtown, where Harold always bought me a coffee and cinnamon bun in the Quality Bakery on Spadina. Those warm summer nights—and cinnamon buns—I'll never forget.

HOW
TO
BUILD
AN
EMPIRE
ON AN
ORANGE
CRATE

But then, when I was fourteen, my dad got sick. After a lifetime of inhaling Honeysuckles, his lungs finally gave in. He went to his bed in the sitting room and, except for getting up to clerk in emergencies, pretty much stayed there the rest of his life. Doc Pearlman did what he could, then finally brought in a specialist and, for the last few months, a live-in nurse. But my father, who'd always been weak, just got weaker.

He was forty-two years old in 1930, when he died one spring night, at 2 A.M.

I remember Mrs. Kalb from the deli down the street coming into the room. She'd just heard the news and was sobbing. She looked at my father, then reached over and gently pulled the Masonic ring from his finger. "Here, Eddie," she said, as she put the ring on mine. "You wear this now. Otherwise, the undertaker will steal it."

The ring is nearly a century old now, its emblem long worn off. But it's never been off my finger.

Still, even if Mrs. Kalb hadn't given it to *me*, no undertaker would have got it. We had no money for an undertaker. The Masonic Order buried my father. Ironically, after all the futile years he'd given in their service, his final service was given by them. A group of my father's Masonic friends arrived at the store in their tiny leather aprons and handled all arrangements.

And the Cohens, amazingly, took care of the mourners. Newcomers to Toronto, they had just opened a fish store down the street. We hardly even knew them. But after the funeral, Mrs. Cohen had prepared a lavish

spread on the table for everyone. The Freemasons, Doc
Pearlman, the nurse, Rabbi Dinkin, Halperin the barber,
the Walls, the Kalbs, the Goldmans, the Brightmans—the
whole neighbourhood in fact—were there to eat, and
remember my dad.

It was that night, I think, it first dawned on me. With
my father gone, I was suddenly the man of the family.

I was in my third year at Central Tech, and enjoying
it. In our Christmas exams, I'd stood second in the class
—my best marks ever. It left my mother in a quandary.
She wanted me to be educated, but didn't know how,
with three kids to feed, she could manage the store alone.
At first she considered moving back to her relatives, in
Washington, then figured it would be too big a burden
on the Menshs and Kornhausers.

When she finally decided to stay in Toronto, the first
thing she did was apply for Canadian citizenship—for
Bob and me as well as herself—since she could then
collect Mother's Allowance from the government. But
even that monthly bonus didn't make ends meet. Besides
raising her family, my mother was working up to eighteen hours a day—and we were still destitute. There was
only one thing I could do. I quit school.

And so, at fifteen years old, I became the proprietor
of a completely bankrupt store.

CHAPTER THREE

Somehow, I ran it for the next nine years. Or it ran me.

The first thing I did was brighten it up. My dad had used only 60-watt light bulbs, and at night the store was gloomy. So I replaced them with 200-watters, and the whole place suddenly shone—*sometimes*. When we couldn't pay the electric bill, Hydro would cut off the power. Customers would be in there at midnight when— Zap!—it would suddenly be pitch-black. Until the bill (plus an extra "reconnection charge") was paid, we'd carry on with candles. Most of my time was spent in the dark anyway. I'd get up at four every morning, bicycle down to the bustling St. Lawrence Market on the water-front or the Farmer's Market miles away on the Humber River to buy the day's fruit and vegetables, and get back by seven to open the store. While my mother clerked, I'd order the bagels, butter, milk, and canned goods, and set prices. When customers asked for credit, I'd mark the prices and items on an order form for them and stick the carbon copies in a Kraft cheese box behind the counter. Each week I'd tally up the totals, then try to collect. *If* they paid, I'd pay our suppliers and wholesalers, who never stopped badgering.

But, as always, our "cash flow" usually ran upstream. I spent hours getting loans from finance companies and arranging overdrafts with Fred Bancroft, the manager of the Bank of Commerce at Dundas and Bathurst—which ate up any income. (A few years ago Fred told me I still owe the bank two dollars on a 1933 overdraft. When I offered to pay up on the spot, he flatly refused. He'd paid it himself, he said, and has the framed overdraft hanging on his wall. He loves pointing out to his pals that "Honest" Ed Mirvish owes him two bucks.)

At thirteen, my brother Bob also quit school to work in the store. He worked mostly at nights, clerking at the counter then closing up at two. It bored him blind, but gave me a few free hours for social life. Yale and I would sometimes catch a sixteen-cent movie at the Duchess (where *Tarzan*, *The Little Tramp*, and Shirley Temple were fast supplanting Doug). Sometimes we'd shoot a few games of pool, or wander over to Shopsowitz's Deli on Spadina (where scores of stars like Hope, Benny, Berle, and Borge later used to go for "Shopsy's" famous corned beef). But mostly we'd just drive around in the ten-buck Oldsmobile we bought.

Well, "drive" might be an exaggeration. The first time we took it down along the Lakeshore, we couldn't figure

HOW
TO
BUILD
AN
EMPIRE
ON AN
ORANGE
CRATE

out why everyone was pointing and yelling at us—till we stopped, looked underneath, and saw the battery dangling by its cables on the street. One rainy night we parked with two girls in a deserted field far out in the suburbs. The car sank to its hubcaps in the mud and wouldn't budge. We had to take the girls home on the streetcar, then go back next day to hire a farmer to haul us out with his horse. Once, when a tire blew, we had to drive home on a rim. We couldn't afford a spare.

The worst experience, though, was the day we drove two girls to Niagara Falls. Passing a peach orchard, I saw a lot of branches hanging over a fence and told Yale to stop. We could stock our stores for free. We were madly plucking peaches and stashing them in the trunk, when I suddenly saw the farmer. He was standing just ten feet away with a furious frown. And a dog. And a shotgun.

The girls both screamed and ran to the car. Yale and I both froze. "What the hell you think you're doing?" snarled the farmer.

"Picking peaches, sir," I said.

"Them there's *my* peaches that you're stealing."

"Well, sir"—I gulped, staring at the gun that was staring at me—"we figured if they were hanging over the fence, they'd be free."

The farmer glowered at me for a full thirty seconds, then said, "Hey . . . don't you have a store on Dundas Street?"

I gave it a moment, then finally said, "Yessir."

"Yeah, it's what I thought. But I see your memory ain't so good."

He could see I was stunned. "Well, I'll tell you somethin' son. I *supply* your store with fruit. Now how would you like it if *I* went down there and stole a bunch of peaches off of *you*."

I felt two inches tall. Sheepishly, we returned his peaches and left.

Yet, although the two girls refused to drive with us again, the farmer kept supplying us, without another word about it. But I never again forgot his face.

While the CNE midway and peach-orchard capers were my major—and equally thwarted—ventures into organized crime, I still consistently ran afoul of the law. Even before quitting school, I'd keep getting hauled into court. Mainly it was because of Ontario's "Blue Laws" at the time. The Lord's Day Act stated emphatically that grocery stores had to stay shut on Sundays.

But most of our customers, to whom the Sabbath was *not* Sunday, *liked* to shop then. It was a day of rest rather than religion, an ideal time to stock up on supplies. Who was I, to whom any sale meant money, to pass them up? I'd let them into the store. And almost every week a cop would catch me. Or I'd be delivering bread or milk on my bicycle, and some cop would nab me again.

So off I'd go to Juvenile Court to stand before Judge Mott. I'd see Judge Mott so often he got to know me personally. "Ahhh, Edwin," he'd say with a sigh, "are you

HOW
TO
BUILD
AN
EMPIRE
ON AN
ORANGE
CRATE

back again?" Or he'd shake his head and murmur, "I don't understand it, Eddie. You *look* so innocent." But he knew I had no money, so a fine would be pointless. And he could hardly send such an innocent kid to jail. So at least every month, for years, we'd meet, and repeat the famous Mott–Mirvish routine.

And it wasn't just for breaking Blue Laws. Once I went into Kalb's Deli next door and bought a five-cent corned-beef sandwich. Then I spotted another sandwich on the table beside me, but no one on the seat. So I ate it, too. I'd just finished wolfing it down when a woman said, "That's *mine!*" But I had only one nickel. Back to court. Or the time I smacked a baseball in the back alley and bonked a woman on the head. "Ahhhh, Eddie," Judge Mott would say, sighing, "you just *gotta* cut this out."

But what really scared me was the time I appeared in an adult court. An Italian girl tore her best dress on a loose nail on our fruit stand. Her family laid a charge. When a cop asked me what name they should sue for payment of the dress, I pointed to the name above the store. I went to court and waited till the judge called out "D. Mirvish," then stood up.

"Are you D. Mirvish?" he asked.

"No, sir," I said. "D. Mirvish is dead."

The judge was furious with the Italians and the cop. The cop and Italians were furious with me. Still, it was impossible to sue my father: "Case dismissed."

Meanwhile, the debts piled up. It was only the tenants who kept us afloat. We still gave credit as my father had—even with customers we knew could never pay. I tried to collect as often as I could, but there were still more chits in the cheese box than coins in the till. Perhaps I should have stuck the unpaid bills on the wall behind our counter, as Rosenberg's grocery did down the street. There they hung, with the names and total debts of the creditors, for the entire neighbourhood to see. Rosenberg's clients paid up more than ours—even if it was due to sheer embarrassment.

Finally, by 1938, we'd hit bottom. I told my mom I was closing the store, and sadly she agreed. She'd been in it every day for thirteen years, longer than any other place she'd ever been. But even *she* knew we couldn't go on.

On the day we closed, the finance company bailiffs came to take what they could, and suppliers came to take back their goods. Or at least what Yale and I hadn't stashed in a garage. (Admittedly, I was a bit of a thief, but I wasn't called "Honest" then.)

That's all I remember. The day was a blur of strange faces. But suddenly they were gone, and the shelves were bare. I shut the front door and locked it. It was the first time the shop had ever been closed before midnight.

CHAPTER FOUR

We kept on living at 788 Dundas. We had nowhere else to go.
And besides, the tenants helped pay the rent. But they
didn't put potatoes on the table. That's why I started
working for Leon Weinstein—the very day after we shut
the shop.

Leon, as I've said, was one of the few local kids who
finally made it big as head of Loblaw's, the giant super-
market chain. His dad had also run a local grocery store,
then formed a company called Standard Wholesalers to
supply other grocers. Leon worked for his dad, and that's
how I met him. Every week he'd come to our shop to
take orders—then come back to hassle for payment. He
was loud and tenacious, but never bullying. I always
found him fair.

It was after he'd started his own chain of Power
Supermarkets that I asked him for a job—even though

I knew there were *no* jobs going. "Leon," I said, "I'll work *any* hours for *any* pay. I'm desperate."

Leon knew, all too well, how disastrous our own store had been. But he never blamed *me*. He figured I was much like him: young, ambitious, and used to hard work. So he hired me. And I worked for him, *hard*, for a year. I started at thirteen bucks a week—which, by the time I quit, had soared to a princely twenty-three dollars. I started at the store at 518 St. Clair Avenue West, where I stocked the fruit stand and served customers. After a week, I was promoted to fruit manager of another store up the street. Before I left, I'd been fruit manager of all eight Power stores.

In the meantime our store on Dundas was sitting empty, which seemed stupid. It was Yale who came up with the dry-cleaning scheme. After graduating from Tech, he'd worked in a knitting mill for two years then switched to his brother-in-law's dry-cleaning plant— which had just laid him off. With his new expertise he suggested we open our own dry cleaners in the vacant shop. We didn't have to do any actual cleaning, he said. Customers would bring in their clothes, and he'd drive them back and forth to the cleaning plant in his second-hand Austin truck. I said it sounded terrific. All we needed was a name. But I'd already thought of one.

The two biggest department stores in the city were Eaton's and Simpson's. "Let's call the place *Simpson's*," I suggested.

HOW
TO
BUILD
AN
EMPIRE
ON AN
ORANGE
CRATE

"*Who's* Simpson?" Yale asked.

"*You* are," I said.

"I *am*?" He snorted. "Since *when*?"

Yale's real surname was Shimkofsky, which was *close*. I said if he simply shortened it and switched a few letters, he'd be "Simpson". Which seemed to make sense. So he had the name legally changed.

Then I took the streetcar down to the Robert J. Simpson store one Sunday, stood across the street from its sign, and copied the name exactly on a piece of paper. We used the identical design on the new sign over our store and painted it on the door of Yale's Austin. And so "Simpson's Service Stores" (even though there was only *one*) opened for business.

Surprisingly, it did pretty well. My sister, Lorraine, by then fifteen, dealt with the customers. She made two dollars a week. Yale drove the clothes to the plant and back—and some weeks made even *more* than two bucks.

I was still working for Leon, of course. But since I still rose every morning at four to buy wholesale fruit and vegetables for the Power store, I had most evenings free to help Yale and Lorraine. And since "Simpson's" was on our premises, it paid the family rent.

Of course, most customers who saw the sign thought we were part of the giant department store. It wasn't long before a furious Robert J. Simpson official showed up at our counter. "You must change your sign," he told me. I asked why.

"Because you're using *our* name," he snapped.

"Waddaya mean?" I said. "The name of the guy who runs this place *is* Simpson. Who's *your* Simpson?"

He couldn't answer. All the department store Simpsons had long since died. It was run by a man named Burton.

"In fact," I told the official, "I think you should change the name of *your* store."

"Yeah?" he said, growing redder. "To *what*?"

"Shimkofsky's," I said.

Our sign stayed up.

But after a year Yale wanted out. At the best he made eight dollars a week. He knew he could make far more. It was 1939—the year *Gone with the Wind* won the Oscar, Douglas Fairbanks passed from life into legend, and World War II began.

Suddenly, ammunition factories were roaring full blast in Toronto, and skilled workers were in demand. So when Yale went to work as a machinist with the H.W. Petrie plant, the Simpson's dry cleaner's closed. My brother Bob was soon to go and join the U.S. Merchant Marine, and Lorraine couldn't run it alone.

It was far from the end of my relationship with Yale, though. In the 1950s we again formed a couple of small plastic-manufacturing companies in a building I'd bought near Honest Ed's on Bloor. And later, in the Royal Alexandra and restaurants, he became my right-hand man. And the man's still there.

Meanwhile, after the dry-cleaning empire's demise, our family finally moved from the Dundas store where

HOW
TO
BUILD
AN
EMPIRE
ON AN
ORANGE
CRATE

I'd spent my youth to a duplex on Page Street, eleven
blocks away. But, except for the storefront, it wasn't much
different. There was a living room, tiny kitchen, and
single bathroom. My mom and Lorraine slept in one
bedroom, Bob and I in the other. But after Bob left home,
I began to share the bedroom with my beautiful
new bride.

I'd first met Anne Maklin three years before when a
mutual friend introduced us. On our first date she
wanted to go to the Royal Ontario Museum. Our second
was at the Silver Slipper on New Year's Eve, 1939, and
we'd courted ever since—mostly by daily mail, however,
since she lived in Hamilton, the famous Steel City just
west of Toronto. Besides being lovely, Anne was tremen-
dously talented; she painted, played piano, and sang so
well that a band leader once asked her to join his group.

Anne's mother, Jennie, like my father, was born in
Russia—and she'd sailed to the New World in 1905, just
two years after my dad arrived. But Jennie was only five
when she came to Canada.

Jennie's father, a French Jew, had been an engineer
with the Russian railroad. One morning as he left for
work his young wife, Ida Pearl, pleaded with him not to
go; she'd had a premonition of great danger. The engineer was not a superstitious man. He'd gone off smiling,
climbed aboard his locomotive, and died that day in a
horrible accident.

But Ida Pearl, suddenly left with a small son and

daughter and her own widowed mother, had amazing Russian grit. After the funeral she went to the palace of Tsar Nicholas II in Kiev, and demanded an audience with the Tsar *himself*. So impressed by her passion were the Kremlin courtiers that they actually ushered her into Nicholas' chambers—where she begged him to be allowed to emigrate to Canada. She had two brothers in Hamilton, Ontario, and wanted to join them. The last ruling Romanov was equally won over. He granted her request.

And so, with her mother and two small children, Ida Pearl left Russia. It was just weeks before the famous sailors' mutiny on the battleship *Potemkin* and the Bloody Sunday massacre in St. Petersburg, which ignited the Revolution.

They settled in Hamilton, where little Jennie grew up, went to business college, and studied piano. At sixteen, she married a handsome young immigrant from Russia named Jack Maklin and bore him two daughters.

But Anne's sister died before she was three, and Anne was raised by her mother and indomitable grandmother who'd once met the Tsar. In Hamilton, Ida Pearl had meanwhile remarried—a kindly man who sold pots and pans and collected rock specimens—but he too died, when Anne was seven. My wife grew up, she says, "in a house of sadness".

But it was also a house of music. Anne's mother played the piano, and her grandmother sang old Russian songs. Anne also sang every day. *Everywhere*. At home,

HOW
TO
BUILD
AN
EMPIRE
ON AN
ORANGE
CRATE

school concerts, public benefits, in choirs and revues, even on the radio with Percy Faith. The celebrated conductor had gone to Hamilton to audition high-school students in a competitive search for "the most promising female voice in Hamilton and vicinity". Anne was sixteen when she entered—and won. Three years later she sang "Deep Purple" with a night-club band in Baltimore. That's when the leader asked her to join them as a soloist. But Ida Pearl was very ill, so Anne returned to Toronto.

From the age of eleven, she'd also painted, and during her teens, took special art courses. But many of Anne's artistic and community activities went into hiatus when she married me and moved into the Page Street duplex in Toronto.

CHAPTER FIVE

I was still working then at the Power store on St. Clair, filling orders, serving customers, and erecting perfect pyramids of pumpkins, cabbages, and melons on display stands. They took hours to build and only moments to demolish, but they made me feel, briefly, like a Pharoah. On Saturdays I worked from eight till six when we closed, then took stock until long past midnight. I was used to long hours so didn't mind them but always wished I was working for myself.

Often I didn't take a streetcar to work; I'd walk. And one day I passed a store for rent, on the south side of Bloor just west of Bathurst. It was small, the fifteen-foot width of two windows and a door, and only twelve feet deep. It was what was called a "lockup store", with no phone, toilet, storeroom, or back door. There were a lot of lockup stores in the area then. The owners would rent them for a month or two to some hustler with goods to

HOW
TO
BUILD
AN
EMPIRE
ON AN
ORANGE
CRATE

sell off quickly. Then the landlords simply locked the store till the next fast-buck artist took it over.

I passed that shop a hundred times. And the more I passed it, the more I thought. The rent was fifty-five dollars a month, and I talked it over with Anne. She had an office position at the time, which she'd taken a month after arriving in Toronto since she couldn't imagine not working. It was her idea to open a specialty shop of our own. Because she'd worked in sales and an office in Hamilton and considered herself a "people person", she said she'd far rather run a shop herself than sit behind a desk. That did it. We rented the little lockup.

We had $175 in wedding-present money, plus her $212 insurance policy, which she said we could cash, and the bank also gave us $202. After paying a month's rent, we still had $322 to buy merchandise.

Since Anne loved fabrics, colour, and design, we decided to specialize in women's sportswear and came up with the name: Sport Bar. Anne designed the sign, with its dancing letters in a jaunty arc, and I cut them out of plywood with a band saw. Then I nailed rows of shelves to the walls and constructed a counter from Masonite. And finally, with our remaining $322, we bought our first stock of women's clothes.

I'd already checked through the garment district on Spadina and figured that a dress costing $6.95 wholesale could be retailed for $12.95. That $6 markup meant a $6 *profit*. I figured the rent at $2 daily, so even if we sold only *one* dress all day, we were still $4 ahead. So, optimistically, we opened.

And, from the first, did amazingly well.

But actually, it *wasn't* so amazing. The timing was perfect. With all of Europe engulfed by then in battle, thousands of teenage country girls were streaming into Toronto to build parachutes, fighter planes, and bombs in the war plants. For the first time ever, they had the money to spend on smart dresses. And they spent.

I'd rush down to Spadina, buy a new batch of skirts, sweaters, dresses, and blouses from the wholesalers, then trundle them back by streetcar to the shop. Meanwhile, Anne was behind the counter every day from 9 A.M. till 11 at night. Sometimes I'd dash out after dark to get her a vegetable plate with poached egg, which she'd eat in a corner while I clerked. The Sport Bar was thriving. But both Anne and I were dead on our feet. Something had to give.

Eventually, it was me. Soon after the shop opened, I gave up my job with Power. Leon asked me to stay, or even work part-time. I was pleased, and grateful, but said no. By then I wanted to work only for myself.

By then I'd also become adept at spotting the huge dress orders that Spadina wholesalers were sending to major department stores, and I'd bargain for a few off the top before they were shipped. After all, I'd grown up with a lot of those garment-district guys. They knew, and admired, my chutzpah. They liked to see a small fry like me get ahead.

HOW
TO
BUILD
AN
EMPIRE
ON AN
ORANGE
CRATE

It was also with the Sport Bar I first started to advertise — both on signs in the windows and by placing small
ads in the papers (costing two bucks, which was all I
could afford). And I ran just one line: "No down payment. Your credit is good at the Sport Bar." Now *why*,
you wonder, would I continue to give credit after my
disastrous lessons at the grocery store? Good question.
But, as I saw it, there were five good reasons.

First: At the time, everyone *else* was selling *only* for
cash — because everybody *had* cash then. And I quickly
decided, in order to stand out, I had to go against the
trend. So the ad line was revolutionary. A real grabber.

Second: Credit suddenly made *sense*, because people
could pay it off. They had *jobs*.

Third: Because the girls in the munitions plants had
money rolling in, they were happy to spend it on clothes
in a hurry. And if they had credit to buy even *more*,
why *not*?

Four: I discovered I could convert the girls' sales contracts into instant cash by selling them, slightly below
their full value, to a finance company. The finance company, having got the contracts at a discount, would then
collect the *full* amount. But I had no worries about anyone defaulting. And, meanwhile, I was putting cash
straight into our bank account.

Five: On Friday paydays, when the factory girls
arrived at the shop to make a payment, I'd tell them I'd
sold their contracts to the Mutual Discount Company.
The girls didn't care, since their payments were the same.

Then, I'd try to sell them another dress—and another contract. And it worked. After two years, we had nearly 10,000 contracts in the system. And everyone was happy.

Meanwhile, since the garment district also gave credit, I'd buy, say, $5,000 worth of dresses for $200 down, with a promise to pay the balance in sixty to ninety days. So, although I was constantly in debt to the wholesalers, I was constantly operating on *their* money.

It was a spiraling business. I'd whip down to Spadina and get new merchandise for the shop, sell it on credit, re-sell the discounted sales contracts to Mutual, then bank the cash—from which I'd send part payments to the wholesalers. And, all the time, I'd be signing up new contracts.

Which shows what a little luck and enterprise can do.

But yet, who knows? I may still have been selling ladies' skirts and sweaters in the Sport Bar—if Dr. William Edward Tindale didn't die when he did.

CHAPTER SIX

Dr. Tindale was our wealthy landlord.

One of his numerous properties in Toronto was the stretch of stores on Bloor running east of Markham Street. Besides our Sport Bar, they included Sophie's Beauty Parlor, Hilda Pepper's Hat Shoppe, Witkin's Optometrist's, and Mike's Shoe Repair. The two floors above each store were crammed with apartments, plus Dr. Turack's dental office. I'd never met Dr. Tindale in person, but paid our rent each month to his equally rich real-estate agent, a cultured gent named W. T. Hambrook with whom I'd become quite friendly.

But I'll never forget the final days of August 1945. We were still cheering the news that Japan had surrendered, when Hambrook phoned to tell me Tindale had just died. I asked him who was getting the Bloor Street strip. "Well," he said, "the doctor left all his property to the

University of Toronto. That particular strip was willed to Trinity College."

I was stunned. "Look, Mr. Hambrook," I said, "could I come and see you?"

"When?" he asked.

"As soon as I can," I said.

So even before the good doctor was buried, I was out at Hambrook's huge house in Oakville to ask if the college was willing to sell. "Good Lord, Ed." Hambrook snorted. "Why are you always hustling so hard? You won't live long yourself if you keep it up."

"I *have* to," I told him. "No one else will hustle *for* me."

Hambrook laughed, and said he'd check it out. He did more than that. He went to the University of Toronto bursar, Mr. Strathy, and pleaded my case himself. I'm sure it helped that the men were old friends. But a few days later Hambrook called to say that Trinity College had no use for the property. I could have it, he said, for $25,000.

"That's a *lot*," I said, choking. "I'll have to go up to my neck in debt."

"I've already taken care of that," said Hambrook. "Give them $5,000 cash, and we'll arrange a $20,000 mortgage with Trinity College."

"Done!" I said. And so it was that five months later, on January 4, 1946, I became the proud owner of an absurdly skinny stretch of buildings on Bloor, running

HOW
TO
BUILD
AN
EMPIRE
ON AN
ORANGE
CRATE

125 feet, 7 inches along the sidewalk—and 12 feet deep.

Actually, we put the property in Anne's name, and nine years later, after Honest Ed's was thriving, transferred it to one of our companies, Davanne Holdings Ltd.

Naturally, I stayed a close friend of W. T. Hambrook for the rest of his life. But every time I saw him he'd shake his head. "For gawdsakes, Ed. Why didn't I buy that property *myself?*"

There've been times I wish he *had*. One was soon after I took it over. For, in order to expand our own tiny shop, I needed the space being used by Mike's Shoe Repair next door. Running forty feet across the front, it was twice as wide as the Sport Bar. The shoe repairman Coco Myles, and his son Lou, who came in after school to shine shoes, were my friends, and the repair shop itself, which had been there for years, was a local landmark. It was terrible telling them they had to go.

At least, after Coco's son gave up shoeshining for tailoring, I bought every suit I own from his famous Lou Myles men's-wear store. But then, so have scores of movie stars.

After expanding the Sport Bar to three times its size, we immediately upgraded our entire line of ladies' wear and renamed the shop Anne & Eddie's. But Anne wasn't there. In July 1945, we'd left my mother and sister Lorraine in the Page Street duplex, and moved into our own brick home at 181 Castlefield Avenue, which we got for $2,500 cash and a $4,500 mortgage.

It was there Anne stayed to raise our baby son,

David, who'd been born on August 29 — the day after Dr. Tindale died.

As I said, it was truly a memorable month. For the first time ever we'd suddenly become not only landlords but parents.

For twelve dollars a week I convinced Lorraine, who'd been working in a bakery, to clerk in our new Anne & Eddie's shop. And when business started growing I hired a girl named Gert Sax (who stayed with me for years) to help my sister. But besides selling more expensive clothes, we'd made one other drastic change from the Sport Bar. All sales were strictly in *cash*.

Once again I'd decided to buck the general trend. During the booming war years, other stores had also started offering credit to the factory girls, and by 1944 the practice had become the norm. But the war was obviously ending. And with it would go the munitions plants, and the hordes of splurging girls who loved to stretch their pay cheques. I figured, correctly, that soon we'd have to cater to new customers. Which is why we upgraded our stock, and also why Anne & Eddie's took cash only.

Since I knew absolutely nothing about decor, I'd go down to study Eaton's and Simpson's stunning window displays, then dash back to create ersatz versions of our own. (For a while, don't ask why, I went wild about displaying all-black dresses against checkered pink-and-black backdrops.) Or I'd send Lorraine to check the displays in the dress shop across the street for new ideas. If we liked them, we used them. I've never had an

HOW
TO
BUILD
AN
EMPIRE
ON AN
ORANGE
CRATE

aversion to creative borrowing. At any rate, whatever we did *worked*! From 9 A.M. till 11 at night, Anne & Eddie's jumped.

There was just one problem.

I'd become sick of selling dresses.

They required too much *service*. And they just weren't *exciting*. I wanted to sell stuff you could simply display and let people pick out for themselves. Like canned beans, for instance, or carrots. Okay, like groceries! Things people want which you don't have to *push*. I was simply tired of catering to customers.

So when I heard of a big fire sale of merchandise from a burned-out Woolworth's store in Hamilton, I bought the entire stock—even though I didn't have a clue what it was. I trucked all the cartons down to Toronto and stored them in our basement. It was sort of like Christmas morning, ripping the boxes open to discover what was in them. It was, of course, typical five-and-dime stuff. Potato peelers. Bird feeders. Egg beaters. Gewgaws. Friends would drop by and pick out trinkets.

Meanwhile, I kept on buying bankrupt stock, distressed merchandise, and job lots. And soon our entire basement was jammed with a few hundred thousand small items—which, I figured, cost a quarter of a cent each. But our store was too small to sell any of it. There was only one painful solution. I had to ask Sophie's Beauty Parlor and Hilda Pepper's Hat Shoppe to relocate.

While we were expanding into the new space, Anne came back to manage our closing sale at Anne & Eddie's.

Three months later, when the stock was gone, I closed the shop and removed the sign from over the door. Anne & Eddie's was out of business. I'd peddled my last petticoat.

Now I was ready to sell those tons of items stored in the basement. And, with all the space once occupied by the Sport Bar, Mike's Shoe Repair, Hilda's, and Sophie's, I had the room to sell it. So we carted everything down to Bloor Street—and displayed it all on orange crates both in the store and on the sidewalk outside.

Finally, I'd found my true forte. Customers could wait on themselves and choose what they wanted. While *I* stayed strictly planted behind the cash register.

But I needed a couple of employees to restock the orange crates and watch for shoplifters. One was my mom, who asked if she could help. Since my sister had just married a soldier named Lazarus and moved to the Yukon where he was stationed, my mother was living alone. Without Lorraine, or a job, she was bored. Besides, she could spot any shoplifter like a hawk. The other employee was Lorraine's new brother-in-law, Morris Lazarus—the first man I ever hired—who spent all week as a travelling salesman but on Saturdays was free.

And that was just dandy with me, for I intended to open the store on Saturdays only. "If I can clear a hundred bucks just one day a week," I told Anne, "I'll close up for the other six." And Saturday was the obvious day because it was always the busiest.

HOW
TO
BUILD
AN
EMPIRE
ON AN
ORANGE
CRATE

And so one morning in the spring of 1948—the year Israel came into existence and Gandhi was shot, to keep it in some historical perspective since my own proud endeavour made not a single headline—I unlocked the front door of my new store.

Over the entrance I'd painted a sign:

NAME YOUR OWN PRICE! NO REASONABLE OFFER REFUSED!

It wasn't as crazy as it sounded, since *any* price over a quarter of a cent was pure profit. When people asked, "Who decides what a reasonable offer *is*?" I'd say, "The honest one. Me."

I'd also run an ad in the papers which I'd scribbled out on our kitchen table. It said:

Our Building is a dump!

Our Service is rotten!

Our Fixtures are orange crates!

But!!!

Our Prices are the lowest in town!

Serve yourself and save a lot of money!

Regardless of the exclamation points—which, like pink-and-black backdrops are one of my weaknesses—the pitches paid off. All that Saturday I accepted cash offers (*always* for more than if I'd priced them), punched the till, and watched a torrent of customers pour in. In a word, we were mobbed.

It was the opening day of Honest Ed's.

CHAPTER SEVEN

So why, as everyone's asked for nearly half a century, did I choose that idiotic name, Honest Ed?

To be honest—as God knows I've *had* to be ever since adopting it—I don't know. It just hit me one day.

I've always hated hypocrisy. And to me, the honorific "honest" always smacked of something shady. If not, why would so many two-bit politicians and snake-oil salesmen use the name? Unless, of course, they were trying to portray themselves as something totally opposite to what they were. It's a name I just found ridiculous.

Which, I think, is why I chose it. I *wanted* to give real deals, but I knew that people were suspicious of bargains that sound *too* good. And most ads I saw in the papers simply *preened* with smugness. So again I opted to buck the trend. Rather than sound self-serving, I decided to take the mickey out of all the usual sales pitches and sanctimonious slogans—and call myself "Honest Ed".

HOW
TO
BUILD
AN
EMPIRE
ON AN
ORANGE
CRATE

I thought it sounded appropriately stupid. And everyone agreed. Few names could be more inane. But I figured if you knocked yourself, you'd get attention. And it did. It *hooked* 'em.

It also provided an unexpected bonus. If your name was "Honest", I discovered, everyone kept an eye on you. Which was fine. Because to *do* so, they *had* to come down to the store. So I've been Honest ever since.

But I also needed a silly face to go with the silly name. Most of my friends said my *own* mug would fill the bill ideally, yet even then I was modest. And meanwhile, I'd found the perfect guy for the role. His name was Dick MacDougal, known to all in the Bloor-Bathurst area as Dirty Dick. The archetypal drunken bum, Dick was skinny, totally toothless, perpetually filthy, with stubbled chin, cauliflower ears, and a corkscrew nose. In return for our letting him sleep in the store's basement, he'd shovel the sidewalk and stoke the furnace when he wasn't guzzling kickapoo juice.

His face was any mother's nightmare. So I had a photographer take a picture of old Dick grinning, then hung a huge blowup over the door with the caption: HONEST ED WELCOMES YOU.

And for years most people thought that Dirty Dick *was* Honest Ed. In fact, as his celebrity grew, he began to believe it himself. Never once did he deny it when strangers in taverns bought him beers or people stopped to shake his hand. Even the cops thought he was me. For whenever he'd get picked up for being drunk and disorderly, they'd phone my mother in the middle of the night and say, "Ma Mirvish, your son is here." And she'd always go down to the Western Hospital or Don Jail and haul him back to his cot in the cellar.

At Christmas I'd dress him up as Santa, and he'd reel through the store going, "Ho, ho, ho." But one year, in his Santa suit he staggered out the door, and stood in the middle of Bloor and Bathurst directing streetcars. That was his last season as Mr. Claus. The following year I hired an ex-convict to play the part.

But Dirty Dick's photo stayed above the door for years. And when I opened my first restaurant, Ed's Warehouse, I hung his mug outside the entrance as well—until Yale Simpson asked me to take it down. "It's spoiling people's appetites," he explained. I did so reluctantly, for I'd always liked the old character. But by then Dick had died—so he couldn't give me hell for removing the picture of the real Honest Ed.

Meanwhile, soon after opening the store, I made a few changes. Because it was taking up too much time, I scrapped the "name your own price" system and began pricing items. Even so, they were still the cheapest in town. And the crowds kept on grabbing them up.

I also soon scrapped my "Saturday-only" policy. I'd become a victim of my own avarice. Business was just too *good* to open up for only one day a week. Soon I was running the store for three days, then five, and finally six. For a guy who'd wanted to work one day a week and relax the rest, greed had got the best of me. And

HOW
TO
BUILD
AN
EMPIRE
ON AN
ORANGE
CRATE

suddenly, I was working harder than ever. But then, look-ing back, I don't know what I'd have done with a six-day holiday anyway.

My mom and Morris Lazarus kept sorting the goods and dumping them onto orange crates, and I'd keep clanging the till on the checkout counter. But while department stores were offering wide aisles, specialized departments, alluring display cases, sales clerks, free delivery, refunds, choices in style and size, and credit cards, I kept on bucking the trend.

We took only cash. Accepted no credits cards or cheques. And gave no service, no delivery, no refunds, no exchanges, no credit, no free parking, no frills. When people came in with an item to return, I'd point to the dozens of signs on the walls: ALL SALES FINAL. When they shouted they were never coming back (although they always did), I'd say, "I'm sorry."

What customers got in return was a dandy deal: *low* prices. What we saved in the usual services, we could turn over to the patrons in reduced costs. There were never any miracles to the store's success. We just stuck to a policy which worked. And nothing much has changed in the half-century since.

Even before I opened "Honest Ed's" I'd decided one thing: I would never again start my working day at 4 A.M. So we opened the store at noon. Again, it was bucking the usual trend of 9-to-5 shopping hours. But even as business grew, and I kept increasing the days we were open, I refused to open early. The sign outside said:

OPEN DAILY 11 A.M., with a line underneath: *Our help sleep in the mornings. They go to parties at night.*

Though opening late was at first due to laziness, I soon realized it was also profitable. With fewer business hours, operating costs were less. Not only that, but people started lining up on the sidewalk to grab the opening bargains, and an excitement was generated through the crowd. Then once inside, after waiting a couple of hours in a queue, they'd race through the aisles in a shopping frenzy. It became a first-come-first-served syndrome.

When we were open only Saturdays, we made about $400 a day. After expanding to five days a week, we were selling about $80,000 worth of goods a year. And within five years, gross sales had zoomed to $2 million annually. By then, Honest Ed's was on the shopping map. And our idiotic slogans, sales promotions, and cheap giveaways were becoming famous.

It started when I found a few dozen prescription glasses in some box I'd bought at a fire sale. But the only thing I knew about prescription specs was that a semi-literate cousin of mine named Sussman, posing as an optometrist, used to peddle them throughout Virginia. And, before the cops finally caught him, I'm sure old "Doc" Sussman had blinded half the state.

So I simply left my glasses in their box and stuck it outside the store with a sign: *Your choice 9 cents.* Minutes later, watching through the window, I saw a woman come by with a small squinting son in tow. She was on her way to Witkin's, the optometrist who—before I

HOW
TO
BUILD
AN
EMPIRE
ON AN
ORANGE
CRATE

cancelled his lease—was still in business on our second floor. Besides the prescription in her purse, the lady had twenty bucks her husband had handed her to get their kid a new pair of glasses.

When she saw my box of specs, the woman stopped. Then she started scooping out handfuls of goggles to compare the prescription numbers on them with her own. Every few seconds she'd slap another pair on the poor kid's nose until, after twenty minutes, he finally blurted, "Hey, Ma, I can *see!*"

I felt as proud as my cousin Doc Sussman must have. Giving new sight to the squinty.

But—and this is important—after shelling out 9 cents for the glasses, the lady spent the remaining $19.91 from her 20 bucks on stuff *inside* the store.

So I did the same thing with my red flannel bloomers. *Twenty thousand pairs*, in fact! I found them in the cellar of a warehouse about to be razed. And, mainly because I've always loved red, I bought the entire batch for less than a penny a pair. Then, like flags festooned on a battleship, I draped them on clotheslines outside the store. The price, since it worked before, was nine cents each.

Women giggled, but grabbed them up. Every single bloomer was sold within three days.

Which gave me the idea of using daily *door-crashers* to lure customers into the store. It instantly became one of my basic business principles. Pull the people in with some real "super-bargain"—sacks of potatoes for a dime, nylons for a nickel — even though you lose money. But once they get inside, they *spend*! And *that's* the bottom line. As a kid in the grocery store, I'd thought business was trying to collect from creditors. It had taken some years to discover that business meant making a profit.

But I never had any *pattern* for development. I'd try something out. If it worked, I'd repeat it. If it didn't, I'd scrap it. Fortunately, most things worked. And it wasn't long until I knew I needed far more space.

So, again reluctantly, I had to terminate the leases of my remaining shop tenants on Bloor, and all the apartments above them. After they'd gone, I knocked down the walls between them and expanded the store into the three vacated floors. But not all the floors were level — or even *on* the same level. Crooked stairs connected the ones that didn't match.

I still insisted the new aisles stay narrow to make room for the heaping display counters. So the interior decor remained Early Caveman, which I loved. But the Bloor Street façade still looked a bit bland. Except for a sign with flashing light bulbs over the entrance saying *This Is Honest Ed's*, there wasn't much else on the old brick wall and I wanted to jazz it up.

As luck would have it — and I've *always* had luck — a couple from Florida just happened to drive past the store at the time, and spying the peeling paint out front came in to see me. Back home, they told me, they did house painting and decorating, but had run short of cash on

HOW
TO
BUILD
AN
EMPIRE
ON AN
ORANGE
CRATE

their vacation. Would I like them to paint the outside of the store?

"That's amazing," I said. "It must be telepathy. I'd like some crazy slogans painted all *over* the front. But I want them *loud*."

So they painted the entire three-storey façade snow white, then added five huge slogans in comic-strip balloons:

Honest Ed's no beauty! Waddya expect at these prices? A movie star?

How cheap can a guy get? Come in and find out.

No sour-faced clerks. Just a little on the homely side.

Honest Ed's where only the floors are crooked.

Behind the plaster curtain the best buys in town.

Then, along the top of the store stretched a giant sign:

HONEST ED'S 4 CROOKED FLOORS OF BARGAINS.

I thought the lines were all pretty catchy. As the scriptwriter, I was pleased as Punch. And newspaper photographers came to take shots of my latest claim to insanity. But the Florida couple weren't quite done.

On the Markham Street side of the store, I also had them write: *If these prices don't satisfy you, waddaya want, BLOOD?* Then all down the white wall and across the sidewalk, they'd painted these huge scarlet blood-like blotches. *This*, I considered their masterpiece. But when I brought Anne down to show her, she took one look and declared it "absolutely disgusting". What's more, she said it made her *nauseous*.

So the very same day as it's grand unveiling, I had to get the artists to paint their magnum opus out. As they slathered white paint across it, I felt slightly nauseous myself. I told them how sorry I was when I paid them off with a bonus, for I knew they felt devastated, too. They climbed in their old car and drove back to Florida. I never saw them again. But I've always hoped this crushing setback didn't stifle their careers.

CHAPTER EIGHT

After our first expansion, business grew apace with the added
space. So I started getting ready for the second. I couldn't
extend the store any further to the rear because the property running behind it was filled with the backyards of
the houses facing onto Markham Street. The only possible way for me to expand any further was to buy
those homes.

So in March 1952 I bought my first Markham Street
house, the one directly behind us. It was 17 feet wide by
125 feet deep, and I bought it from a lady named Violet
Broad for $18,000 cash. In the next few years I kept on
buying—seven more houses until I had a total frontage
on Markham of 134 feet, plus the lots behind, for which
I'd shelled out $170,000 in cash and mortgages.

To me, in the early fifties, that was still big money—
considering that, just eleven years before, we'd had to
scrape up $377 to open the tiny Sport Bar. But then, that

My mother and father,
David and Anna Mirvish,
1912.

Me, aged seven,
with cousin Edith,
Washington, D.C.

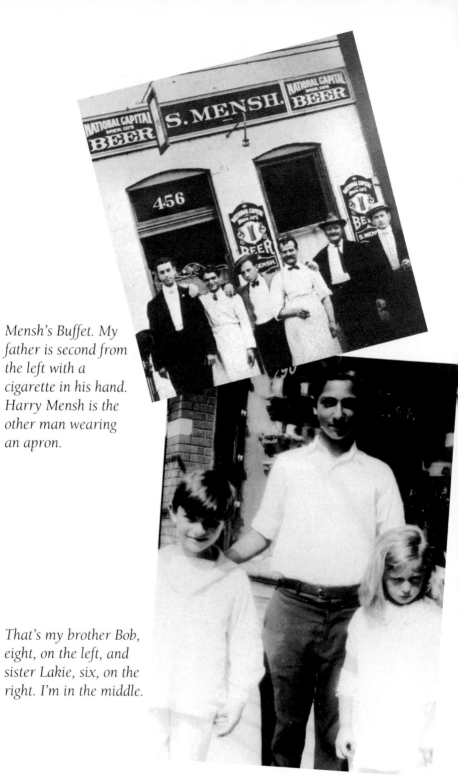

Mensh's Buffet. My father is second from the left with a cigarette in his hand. Harry Mensh is the other man wearing an apron.

That's my brother Bob, eight, on the left, and sister Lakie, six, on the right. I'm in the middle.

With Yale at the Sunnyside bathing pavilion about 1930.

*My mother and I, behind the counter
in the store on Dundas Street, Toronto.*

Anne and me on our wedding day.

PROMOTIONS...

...up to 7,000 people lined up for bargains in the 1950s

...the "Wilderness Girl" mushed from Canada's north country to park her team in front of the Bloor Street emporium

..."Santa's daughters" smiled for the cameras

...the store stayed open day and night for 72 hours during the dance marathon

AND MORE PROMOTIONS...

...I was the only adult raised by my wife and our son

...lying down on the job

...you gotta love those bargains!

Princess Diana at the Royal Alex, 1991.

The Queen Mum opens the Old Vic, 1983.

Opening night at the Princess of Wales Theatre, 1993.

There's no sign anywhere quite like it: 23,000 light bulbs light up Bloor Street.

Over 25,000 attended my seventy-eighth birthday celebration, 24 July, 1992.

dinky little dress shop made it possible to buy all the other properties we've purchased since—including the store, Mirvish Village, the restaurants, the theatres. Without it, the Royal Alexandra might well today have been a parking lot.

Yet, since *nothing* I've ever purchased has been purely altruistic, I bought the houses on Markham only to expand Honest Ed's. And although I rarely plan ahead, I considered this move a good one.

But *then*, having purchased half the block, I discovered to my horror that Markham was zoned "R"—which meant for "residential use" only. The only place I could do any business, it appeared, was my original fifteen-foot-wide Bloor Street strip. Terrific!

So I looked up Lewis Duncan, an absolutely brilliant if unconventional lawyer who had once been a city councillor, nearly became mayor, and loved to fight the system. He sounded like my kind of lawyer. And he was. Duncan discovered that the zoning bylaw said no commercial property could "abut" Markham. So he suggested that if I sold off a narrow strip of my land that stretched along the sidewalk to someone else, I could expand the store onto the property *behind* the strip.

And that's exactly what I did—then later bought it back.

In the interim, the city's zoning experts had taken us to court. But Lewis Duncan came through again, finding another loophole in the bylaws. The man had a truly

HOW
TO
BUILD
AN
EMPIRE
ON AN
ORANGE
CRATE

amazing mind, and I was deeply saddened when a few years later he shot himself to death. To expand the store I knocked down all the houses that I'd bought, and simply connected the new four-storey section to the old one — which gave us 65,000 square feet of selling space on all four floors. I also fireproofed the entire building, and added a $100,000 sprinkler system connected to the fire department. When it was finally installed, I dangled signs around the walls: LOOK! AT LAST! HONEST ED'S HAS RUNNING WATER!

The Official Grand Opening Sale was on October 23, 1958. We jammed Honest Ed's with clowns and brass bands, ran dozens of spot sales, gave away hundreds of silver dollars, and sent two kids racing through the aisles to pile as many toys as they could onto wagons. The kids got prizes. The Sally Ann got the toys.

We got scads of free print. And four months later, we got far more. That's when we unveiled the World's Largest Readograph on the Markham Street side — a mammoth 20-by-135-foot changeable letter sign with the smallest letters stretching ten feet tall. It had 4,800 feet of neon tubing, 1,500 copy panels, and took ten men and two boom trucks to get it up. For twenty-four hours a day it flashed with the words "Save $ Save $ Save $" racing around its borders. It cost $650,000, but was worth every penny in promotions and free publicity.

The initial publicity was instant, if unexpected. Mayor Nathan Phillips (whom the vast square in front of Toronto's City Hall is named for) was there for the unveiling. It was the night of February 12, 1959. The crowd cheered wildly when the sky above glowed as Mayor Phillips pushed the button to light the giant Readograph—and all the houses on Markham Street went black. As well as all the lights on Palmerston, the next street over. In fact, the sudden power failure blacked out the whole area—except for the furiously flashing World's Largest Readograph.

Well, *that* hit the papers next morning.

By then I'd already discovered that even one free story is always worth a thousand paid ads. They reach readers who don't even *look* at ads. And don't cost a cent. So I decided to keep on hustling for as many more as I could. And for that precise purpose, I had hired Bob Gray as our publicist.

Bob was a six-foot-two, 230-pound freelancer from Brooklyn who loved new stunts and well-aged Scotch—with which, as a stimulus to his creativity, he constantly consorted. And, while many of Bob's whacky schemes proved disastrous, the ones that worked were brilliant. The first he dreamed up was in 1957, when he had me stand outside the Fred Victor Mission on Christmas Eve and hand out dollar bills to the jobless.

As the news swept up and down Jarvis Street, hundreds of the homeless swarmed to the mission. I passed out $325 in two hours. It got many men rooms on that icy night, and a front-page story in the *Star*. (Since then, however, I've contributed to the Mission privately.)

The following year we put on the "Triplets Fashion

HOW
TO
BUILD
AN
EMPIRE
ON AN
ORANGE
CRATE

Show", in which twenty-one sets of triplets modelled clothes from Honest Ed's, and the "Bring Back the Prices of the '30s Sale" where we sold bread for a nickel and ten pounds of spuds for seventeen cents, and "The Great Coffee Sale" (after I'd read in a Florida paper during a holiday that coffee prices were going up and phoned the store to make coffee a door-crasher) when crowds lined up around the block to buy a dollar jar for twenty-three cents. That story even made the AP wire and ran in papers across the continent.

Bob Gray stunts like that went off without a hitch. But then there were others. They got us big press, but nearly gave me ulcers. Like the time he dreamed up the idea of me giving the first Toronto baby born in 1958 its weight in silver dollars. But the mother of the first baby, born smack at midnight in Grace Hospital, wanted no part of the promotion.

"Well, we *tried*," I told Bob.

"Hey, don't give up," he snorted. "We'll give the bread to the *second* kid born."

So on the first of January at the East General Hospital, there I stood at the bedside of Mrs. James G. Sullivan who'd had a daughter at 12:12 A.M. The baby was there, along with the scale to weigh it, and the photographers. The only thing Bob had forgotten were the silver dollars. I turned as red as the bawling baby.

Fortunately Bob's bright young assistant, Lorraine Messinger, was there. Racing home, she bought over her own father's collection of silver dollars (at considerable profit to her dad), and the weighing ceremony went on within the hour. I gave Mrs. Sullivan $160 for her baby's education, and the hospital another $160 for its building fund. But the photos and stories which ran on all front pages next day focused mostly on the mother, the baby, Lorraine—and her dad's silver-dollar collection.

Yet fiascos didn't seem to faze Bob Gray. What mattered to him was only the sheer originality, the *magnitude* of each promotion. And I must give him credit. He was great at spawning new and ever bigger stunts, even though most were like grabbing a Bengal tiger by the tail.

And he actually *did*, one July, want me to include a tiger in our giant "Noah's Ark Sale". That was the time our carpenters built a giant wooden ark in the store's basement (after our janitor, Dirty Dick, had gone on to direct new streetcars in the hereafter) and filled it with squirrel and spider monkeys, honey bears, a coatimundi (which resembles an anteater, but hates ants), and a California sea lion named Daffy. The animals were the lure.

What we really wanted was to sell the thousands of items of lawn furniture displayed across 18,000 square feet on the two floors above—where, like the Dream sites, we also offered spot specials. One policeman's wife in the right spot got a mink stole for $1.98. Another lucky lady bought a $177 lawn-furniture set for $1.77. And amazingly, some customers even bought the monkeys.

The Noah's Ark Sale extended three days. At the end of it every lawn chair was gone, but I still had a cellar full

HOW
TO
BUILD
AN
EMPIRE
ON AN
ORANGE
CRATE

of animals—plus an absolute mess. So I held a cheap snap auction to find proper homes for the poor critters.

But after that particular promotion, even *I* wasn't happy, no matter how much we'd made on the furniture. Like the Scott Mission stunt, it clawed at my conscience to use hapless people, or animals, for publicity.

Unfortunately, no one wanted Daffy. When he caught a cold we called a vet to take him away, but somehow the little sea lion escaped. And amazingly he flippered his way, unseen, for ten miles east of the city. Presumably he'd followed the railroad tracks—because that's where a freight train hit him. The story made every paper. But it didn't make me proud.

Yet while Bob's insane publicity stunts carried on into the sixties, I finally had to let him go. There was only one person to replace him, of course. Lorraine Messinger became my chief publicist.

CHAPTER NINE

After I bought the houses on Markham Street to extend the store, I just kept on buying—right down the block.

If it seems I was trying to imitate my uncle, Harry Mensh, who purchased half the property in Colonial Beach, I wasn't. I bought the houses to build a parking lot for Honest Ed's customers. And it wasn't even my idea. It was Harold Menzies'.

Menzies was a portly politician who happened to be a city alderman in my ward. One night in 1959, during a seventy-two-hour Dance Marathon we threw in Honest Ed's, it took Harold forty-five minutes to drive past our store along Bloor. What's more, he'd counted fifteen cops in a five-block stretch sorting out the traffic snarl—"A waste of time and taxpayers' money," he thundered to the press.

Furthermore, said Menzies, traffic to the store was *constantly* congesting the neighbourhood. It actually

HOW
TO
BUILD
AN
EMPIRE
ON AN
ORANGE
CRATE

moved through the area faster in *rush* hours than during *store* hours. And Harold was right. It *did*. So in October 1960, after he'd persuaded City Council to adopt a report that "Mirvish Enterprises be requested to provide an off-store parking lot with a 200-vehicle capacity," Harold and I had a chat. I asked him exactly where he thought the parking lot should be.

"Well, Ed," he said, "you've already bought half a block on Markham. Buy the *rest*, and put it there." It made sense.

But I didn't have time to go out buying houses, so I put Yale Simpson in charge. I told him to pay, within reason, whatever he had to. And Yale was terrific. The first thing he did was buy the city-owned lane behind the store for $29,299, then another twelve houses for a total of $354,500. Though it sounds simple here, his efforts were Herculean.

As were my costs. But we had the land for the parking lot—which I was all set to pave. There was just one hitch, as there always was. The street was still zoned "R" for residential—which didn't, as I suddenly discovered, include parking lots. All I had was the adopted report of October 1960, which was neither a formal guarantee, nor agreement for a zoning change.

Meanwhile Alderman Menzies, who'd instigated the whole parking plot in the first place to appease his constituents, had been drummed out of office in the 1961 elections. And that brilliant lawyer Lewis Duncan, when I desperately needed him, was dead. So I spent countless

hours myself trotting down to City Hall, begging the
Buildings and Development Committee to rezone
the block.

When the committee called a public meeting to discuss it, the same local residents who'd once demanded
the parking lot to ease traffic had decided it would mar
the neighbourhood. Alderman Joe Piccininni, a banana
importer who, at 300 pounds, was amply filling the seat
vacated by Menzies, was the most vociferous opponent.
The committee voted against the parking.

Then Toronto City Council overruled the committee,
and said while I couldn't tear down any houses, I could
put a small lot in *behind* them. But even if I had one
paved, I was still left with all those houses.

I'd never intended to install an artists' colony on
Markham Street, or Mirvish Village as it's now officially
named. Like most things I've gotten into, it just *happened*.
It started when Anne was looking for a new studio to
sculpt and paint in. Then the Gerrard Street Village, a
downtown cluster of painters' studios, crafts shops, and
art galleries, was suddenly levelled—for a new Toronto
General Hospital *parking lot*—and needed a place to
relocate.

So Anne and the other artists, like the celebrated gallery owner Jack Pollock, moved into the houses. We renovated every building and, at Anne's suggestion, painted
them all in pastel colours, yellow, pink, and robin's egg
blue. And soon other sculptors, painters, and shopkeepers started leasing space as well.

HOW
TO
BUILD
AN
EMPIRE
ON AN
ORANGE
CRATE

As I watched the renovations one day with Yale Simpson on the sidewalk, he said, "You know, Ed, a one-sided street doesn't look as good as a two-sided street." And I said, "You're *right*." So back out he went, and for $325,500, bought all twelve houses on the *west* side of Markham. We cleaned, remodelled, and painted every one of those, too.

And soon the entire block of twenty-three houses was alive and humming with studios, galleries, shops, and restaurants. Besides Anne's studio and Pollock's gallery, there were antique, Eskimo, handicraft, movie-poster, earthenware, woollen, art-supply, and comic-book shops, two French restaurants, a café offering Hindu teacup reading, a glass blower—and our son's David Mirvish Gallery, the largest private art gallery in the country and one of the most influential.

Certain politicians, for many years, continued to give us problems with the zoning—to say nothing about the noise. But the village is still there—with even a few of the original tenants—and has now been proclaimed an official Toronto tourist attraction.

Again, the village, like most things we've gotten into, was totally unplanned. It all began because some alderman thought I should have a parking lot.

But, like a once-scruffy child that we've watched grow up and take on a pulsing life of its own, we're proud. Anne still works in her studio there. David has a magnificent art bookstore on Markham Street. I still leave my office to stroll its sidewalks.

And because its residents are far less tenants than next-door neighbours, we're thrilled that the city officially designated it "Mirvish Village". For we love the street, and the people on it. I'd even live there if they'd let me.

CHAPTER TEN

As a kid on Dundas Street, the only legitimate theatre I was even aware of was the Standard down the street on the corner of Spadina and Dundas. Jewish shows came up from New York to play there on the weekends, and the theatre gave free passes to merchants who hung playbills in their windows. I used to put their posters up, but I gave the passes to customers. I *worked* every Friday and Saturday night.

By 1960, the theatre had changed its name to the Victory Burlesque Theatre and—while a decade later the strippers stripped off *everything*—the girls on stage at the time were still required to stay warm in a G-string and pair of pasties. And suddenly, although I'd never been in it as a youth, I became very interested in the Victory. Not because of the shows, but because it was for sale. I thought, besides certain ties with my childhood neigh-bourhood, that it might just be a good buy.

So I brought in a theatre expert named Hack from New York to advise me. He told me if I intended to replace the strippers with legitimate shows the Victory would cost too much to renovate.

"But," he said before leaving, "if you still want to buy a theatre, and the Royal Alexandra ever comes on the market—go for it. It's a sweetheart!"

And just two years later, the Royal Alexandra was for sale. And not only that, but at a *fantastic* bargain!

In 1907, it cost one of Canada's richest men a staggering $750,000 to build.

In 1962, while still considered one of the continent's finest theatres, it was up for sale at the asking price of $215,000. Just incredible!

The young man who built it was Cawthra Mulock, scion of two rich and illustrious old Toronto families, the Cawthras and Mulocks. An early Cawthra led troops against the Americans in the Battle of Queenston Heights. Another made a fortune by importing apothecary goods from New York. By compounding the interest, William Cawthra turned the fortune into millions.

The Mulocks had made their wealth and reputation in the military, law, politics (one led the Clear Grit Party), and an iron works. When Sir William Mulock, a Justice of the Supreme Court of Ontario, married a Cawthra, the famous names finally merged with the birth of their son, Cawthra Mulock. Cawthra inherited a substantial amount of money, bought a seat on the stock exchange, and doubled his inheritance in short order.

HOW
TO
BUILD
AN
EMPIRE
ON AN
ORANGE
CRATE

Cawthra loved the theatre. Especially the magnificent Princess on King Street which specialized in musicals. But one night, when he couldn't buy seats for a hit show at the Princess, the petulant Cawthra said he'd never suffer such abuse again. He would build his *own* show palace on King Street, dammit! And immediately commissioned a rising young architect, John Lyle, to build him "the best theatre in the world".

The Belfast-born, Toronto-bred architect was thrilled. At nineteen he'd studied at the Ecole des Beaux Arts in Paris and had just returned to Toronto the year before. He had as his site the former cricket field of Upper Canada College, which had recently moved north to Oriole Parkway: a lot 100 feet wide by 185 deep.

Surrounded by Doyle's Hotel-Tavern, St. Andrews Presbyterian, and the lieutenant-governor's mansion, the street corners which the former schoolground abutted were called "Education, Legislation, Salvation, and Damnation". John Lyle was determined to add supreme Dignification to the list. After all, Cawthra Mulock had instructed him to "spare no expense towards perfection. Use only the finest materials available, anywhere." And John Lyle did.

For the new Royal Alexandra (named after King Edward VII's wife), he built thirty-inch-thick walls of concrete boned with steel, and faced them with great blocks of sandstone. He used rich cherry wood, walnut, and oak for panelling. He shipped silk tapestry in from France, and the finest marbles from Italy. He imported

French artisans to mould the plaster friezes (while designing all the Louis XVI woodwork details himself). He hung an enormous electric crystal chandelier from a huge but delicate plaster rosette. And since the French Renaissance style was then the rage in Europe, that's what Lyle favoured for both auditorium and façade, with its French mansard roof above the grand lobby.

It was all incredibly exquisite—but Cawthra Mulock wanted even more. He wanted *uniqueness*. So Lyle installed the first air-conditioning in any theatre in North America. While in winter fresh air was drawn over two cast-iron boilers for heat, in summer a crew of men shovelled tons of ice into great basement tanks—then powerful fans sucked air across the ice and blew it up beneath the auditorium seats. Crude as it was, it kept temperatures down to sixty-five degrees even in sweltering city heat.

Lyle also made the Royal Alex the first fireproof theatre on the continent—with a giant asbestos curtain, fireproof exits, and escape routes to clear the building in 150 seconds, plus a huge water tank on the roof holding 12,900 gallons.

It was also the first theatre in North America to use the cantilever principle—thus eliminating all unsightly pillars which had always supported balconies. This alone revolutionized theatre architecture.

About the only thing the theatre *didn't* have was a bar. A *tearoom* yes, but no hard stuff. In 1907, it was still

HOW
TO
BUILD
AN
EMPIRE
ON AN
ORANGE
CRATE

"Toronto the Good". Women weren't even expected to leave their seats during intermission.

So on opening night the crowds stood and cheered—both Cawthra Mulock and John Lyle—*before* the curtain went up. They even cheered the curtain, emblazoned with the royal emblem—to which the theatre had been granted the patent by Alexandra herself.

And over the years they kept cheering as the world's great stars played its stage. Orson Welles, Paul Robeson, the Marx Brothers, Katharine Cornell, Jessica Tandy. All the famous Sirs, including Forbes-Robertson, Lauder, Richardson, Mills, Hardwicke, and Gielgud, and the Dames (Edith Evans, Sybil Thorndike, Judith Anderson). The Lunts, the Barrymores, and Bankhead. The celebrated Canadians: Mary Pickford, Marie Dressler, Bea Lillie, Margaret Anglin, Fay Wray, May Irwin, Hume Cronyn, Raymond Massey, Walter Huston. And such cinema stars as Lillian Gish, Theda Bara, George Arliss, Katherine Hepburn, Julie Harris, Deborah Kerr, Tyrone Power, and Yul Brynner.

And *all* of them loved it. "This is the only theatre that makes my voice sound better than I think it does," said Al Jolson, the man whose dad circumcised me. Even America's most famous stripper, Gypsy Rose Lee (who was starring in the *Threepenny Opera*), said, "The Alex is the most beautiful, delightful theatre I know. It would break my heart if anything happened to it."

And suddenly this historic theatre, which architects, actors, and the public all loved, was up for sale. The

Cawthra Mulock Trust, which owned it, needed money, and was determined to sell it off.

None of the city's other theatre companies had the cash to buy it. The city itself, which already owned the O'Keefe Centre, wasn't interested. Toronto Hydro, which *did* want to buy it, was refused because they wanted to raze it for a parking lot. Any other potential buyers had the same plans for it.

Meanwhile, Anne and David had always loved the theatre. And I had always loved bargains. It seemed like a perfect situation to warrant a Mirvish bid. So we did. But first I sent a broker to negotiate with Gordon Perry, the lawyer in charge of the Cawthra Mulock Trust, without mentioning my name. When, after a few visits he failed to make much headway, I called on Gordon Perry myself.

"But why," he asked, "didn't you tell us *yourself* that you wanted the theatre?" he asked.

"Because," I told him, "I didn't think you'd want to sell to someone called Honest Ed."

"Not at all, Ed," Perry said, smiling, "not at *all*."

And so, on February 15, 1963, we bought the Royal Alexandra for $200,000 cash.

But the deal wasn't quite that simple. The major condition of sale was our promise not to raze it—but continue to run it as a legitimate theatre for at least five years. After this time, if we couldn't sustain it as a theatre, we could convert the building and property into whatever use we chose.

Yet my statement that "it will always be a theatre,

HOW
TO
BUILD
AN
EMPIRE
ON AN
ORANGE
CRATE

even if I have to run it as a loss," made countless sceptics chuckle. Still, I *meant* it. And to prove it, we immediately spent more than double the purchase cost just to *restore* it. Though the renovations were essential from both a business and an esthetic standpoint (since "The Grand Old Lady of King Street" had become pretty smudged and seedy through the decades), we also wanted, somehow, to make Cawthra Mulock and Peter Lyle *proud*.

We hired an interior decorator named Herbert Irvine and, as architects, Allward and Guinlock. The elderly Allward, ironically, was actually *part* of the existing theatre. More than sixty years before, a famous artist named Challener had painted the mural of Venus discovering Adonis above the Royal Alex proscenium. And one of the models Challener had used was a ten-year-old boy named Allward, who later became a renowned architect.

At first I had doubts about Irvine the decorator. I couldn't talk to him. He'd stride through the theatre, snapping off instructions—"We need this colour here, and that material there!"—and then he'd fly off to Venice for three months. But he *was* the right man. The work got done quickly, with exquisite taste.

The tearoom became a most elegant bar. We filled it and the lobby with sixteen pieces of our Louis XV furniture—chairs, sofas, mirrors, petit-point coverings, damasks. We laid 2,000 yards of woven-wool broadloom, ran new carpeting to the second balcony, and hung one ton of hand-made crimson curtains cut from 350 yards of velvet. The auditorium took 500 gallons of antique white paint along with 350 rolls of imported French Baroque flock wall covering.

The new stage curtain, made from 350 yards of fire-proof crimson velvet, weighed 1,000 pounds. The grand old chandelier was replaced with a new one in the French Empire style with more than 8,000 prisms. Every seat was tossed out for new ones, foam-filled and uphol-stered in velour. We took 400 photographs and prints of famous past performers that we'd found, matted them in red, framed them in gold, and hung them in the lobbies and on staircase walls.

Finally, we erected a new marquee out front with 1,362 flashing light bulbs, then arrayed every usher in new maroon jackets, brocade vests, and black-satin trousers.

A lot of sweat, passion, and talent went into that the-atre. Plus an amazing amount of love.

The gala reopening was on Monday, September 9, 1963. Before the show we hosted a dinner for seventy guests, mostly Broadway performers, at Winston's Grill on King Street.

Then, after swarming en masse to the theatre, we were greeted by two sky-stabbing searchlights, a horde of TV cameramen greedy for 11 P.M. newsbites, reporters, photographers, and politicians, including the mayor. Celebrities in the audience included everyone from Wayne and Shuster to Lady Eaton who wrote me later, saying "I can quite honestly say there is nothing in Vienna, Rome, Milan, Paris, London, New York, or

HOW
TO
BUILD
AN
EMPIRE
ON AN
ORANGE
CRATE

Chicago that begins to compare with the charm that is the Royal Alexandra."

Anne was escorted to the opening by Earl Rowe, then the Lieutenant-Governor of Ontario. (Later she sculpted the bronze bust of another such dignitary, former Lieutenant-Governor Keiller MacKay, which has a place of honour in the Mezzanine Lounge.)

During the intermission, actress June Havoc went on stage to praise the theatre. She described its past glories and new, refurbished merits. At the end she pointed to the audience and said, "But most of all, it has *you*. Love it back, and deserve it." The entire room stood and cheered.

In fact, about the *only* thing that received few cheers that night was the stage production, a comedy called *Never Too Late* with William Bendix. Though the critics acclaimed the theatre as magnificent, they suggested it was never too late for the play to end its run.

And thus was my baptism in theatre ownership.

CHAPTER ELEVEN

While the four corners near the Royal Alex were dubbed
Education, Legislation, Salvation, and Damnation when
it was built, only "Salvation" remained when we bought
it. With the college, tavern, and lieutenant-governor's
residence gone, Saint Andrews alone still stood—leaving
the immediate area somewhat bereft not only of laughs,
but nourishment. Doyle's Hotel, while damned, had at
least served food. And theatre-goers like to dine.

Which gave me the idea of opening a dining room.
From a profit standpoint, it seemed to make sense. From
a personal viewpoint, it seemed *insane*. Our store had
prospered by purposely *avoiding* service—which I'd
always considered profit-consuming. Yet any restaurant
which *doesn't* give service is dead. It is, in fact, the *ulti-mate* service business.

So I consulted all the top restaurateurs, from Harry
Barberian, who ran two top Toronto steak houses, to

HOW
TO
BUILD
AN
EMPIRE
ON AN
ORANGE
CRATE

Vincent Sardi of the famous Sardi's in New York. Everyone advised against it. It's a high-risk business to begin
with, they said. And besides, I knew absolutely *nothing*
about running a restaurant. I told them I knew nothing
about running a theatre, either, but they were right.

And yet, as I suggested to Yale Simpson, we could *still*
provide pre-show meals in the theatre itself if we kept
them *simple*. "True," he said, "but where would we *serve*
them?" He had a point. Cawthra Mulock had seen no
need for large lobbies, since gentlewomen never left their
seats. And the tearoom was no bigger than the lobbies.
There was simply no space for a restaurant in the place.

So once again without previous plan, one purchase
of property led to another. I bought the six-storey building next door. It was a plain but solid old dry-goods
warehouse, full of stored furniture, publishers' stock, and
basement printing presses, and belonged to a man
named Aziz. After some stiff bargaining, I finally got the
place for $525,000 cash. And immediately set about
designing a new eating joint for the first floor.

I say "joint" because that's what I *wanted*. One of my
favourite restaurants in the world is Durgin-Park in Bos-
ton, a century-old, rough-and-tumble truck-drivers tavern, where burly guys in visored caps plunk down at
long tables beside pin-striped executives and sink their
shoes in the sawdust. I wanted to duplicate Durgin-Park.
But somehow the sawdust got lost in the shuffle.

I brought in a restaurant designer who studied the
first floor and drew up plans for an Arborite-lined

restaurant with indirect lighting. It would seat 150, and cost $150,000. An interior decorator also drew designs which entailed tearing down all the rows of supporting pillars standing fourteen-feet apart—at $5,000 per pillar. He also wanted chairs costing $65 each. I paid the experts for their time, and said we'd design and decorate the place ourselves.

For the construction we used all our carpenters, electricians, and maintenance men. We lined the kitchen walls with stainless steel from floor to ceiling and raised every oven off the floor so we could clean beneath them daily. The kitchens are still so spotless you could perform brain surgery in them. But *hey*, I have to eat in the place myself. And I'm particular!

For the furnishings we used all the things we'd collected from auction sales and antique stores over the years. Stained-glass windows from demolished buildings, Tiffany-style lampshades with red fringes we'd paid twenty-five to fifty dollars for, scores of Crippled Civilian and Salvation Army chairs at five dollars each, thousands of framed photos of old stage and movie stars found in the theatre, and marble statues of angels.

During the decorations I got a call from an antique dealer, who said she had a pair of stained-glass windows for sale. I went down, liked them, and asked the price. She said, "Eight hundred dollars," and I said, "too much."

She sighed. "You know, it's Saturday afternoon and I haven't made a sale all day." I looked around, then asked how much she wanted for everything in the shop.

HOW
TO
BUILD
AN
EMPIRE
ON AN
ORANGE
CRATE

She said, "Ten thousand dollars," and I said, "I'll take it." We used every single piece in the restaurant.

That's how we decorated it. The final effect, as one writer put it, was "Baroque bordello". It still looks the same today. Outside we hung a sign surrounded with flashing light bulbs. Considering what the building was, the name of the restaurant was totally apt: *Ed's Warehouse*.

There were other signs on the freshly painted white wall outside, saying, "If You Like Home Cooking, Eat At Home", and "Duncan Hines Never Ate Here. He Couldn't Get A Seat". With my usual modesty, the final one read: "World Famous!"

The opening day was January 20, 1966—and, for us, incredibly low key. Not a searchlight nor star in sight. The main reason was that we still didn't have our liquor licence—which arrived exactly ten minutes before we opened the doors at 5 P.M. The other was obvious. We didn't want the press or public finding out that we *still* knew nothing about running a restaurant. And the reason we didn't was simply that we'd never *run* one.

It wasn't like buying a theatre and presenting a show —which other people wrote, produced, and performed in. A restaurant meant starting your own script from scratch, producing every aspect from soup to set design, and directing every performance from dishwasher to maître d'.

But, for dozens of reasons I'll get into later, it worked! Business was brisk from the start, as it *should* have been.

For the food was excellent, and the prices—just like the store—were real bargains. An English cut of roast beef (with rolls, kosher dills, mashed potatoes, Yorkshire pudding, and peas) cost $3.15. Patrons started lining up on the street outside.

Since only half of the room was used, we opened up the entire floor. Soon we opened half of the second floor, and started serving steaks—and then the other half of *it*, as a separate room, which we called Ed's Folly. That gave us a total of 850 seats. And the patrons kept queuing. So we opened the entire basement and called it Ed's Italian. By then we were up to 1,300 seats, and the people kept on packing in.

Since the business was spreading west along King, we decided to just keep going. We'd already gone to the end of the block, so we crossed Duncan Street and bought the next building over. It was the old Lumken-heimer-Morrison Brass Foundry, another six-storey structure on the corner, and we bought it in 1973 for $525,000. That's the building we put Old Ed's in, which brought our seating up to 2,150. That number jumped to 2,430 when we added Ed's Seafood in the basement.

But amazingly, as the restaurants increased, the crowds did as well. So once again I said, "Westward Ho!" and bought the six-storey building next to Old Ed's. There was already a restaurant in its basement, run by someone else. After it went broke, we took it over too. Since we'd already run the gamut of roast beef, seafood, and Italian specialties, we decided to switch to

HOW
TO
BUILD
AN
EMPIRE
ON AN
ORANGE
CRATE

Chinese—and that's where we opened Most Honourable Ed's.

One of the culinary experts I'd initially consulted about opening a restaurant came to me years later and apologized for his pessimism. I simply told him, "Listen, I asked *everyone*! And when they *all* said no, I went ahead." I think I enjoy bucking the experts just as much as proving them wrong.

Ed's Warehouse opened with 192 seats. Today all six restaurants hold 2,600 diners. On busy evenings we serve 6,000 meals. And that's not even including lunch.

Our restaurant complex on King Street today is one of the most successful in the world.

CHAPTER TWELVE

The Old Vic is called the most famous theatre in the world.

Ever since buying the Royal Alexandra I'd heard stories about it. Ralph Richardson and John Gielgud told wonderful tales of their early years of training on its stage, while Peter O'Toole would run on about it for hours. All of them loved it. So did my wife and son.

But when we bought it, I had never seen it. I'd never even been to London.

The fact we took it over was entirely due to Bert Stitt. Bert is a lawyer dealing with clients around the world who had helped us purchase the Royal Alexandra. He knew all our business was confined to two relatively small sections of Toronto around Bloor and King streets.

So when he phoned me on June 8, 1982, he said, "I know you've always balked at branching out, Ed, so you may not be interested. But I've just seen an ad that the Old Vic's up for sale."

HOW
TO
BUILD
AN
EMPIRE
ON AN
ORANGE
CRATE

"How much do they want?" I asked, always curious about theatre costs.

"There's no set price," he said. "It's going to the highest bidder."

"But how can I bid," I said, "when I have no idea how much the place is *worth*," Bert said he'd try to find out. When he called back he told me he'd learned that the theatre governors were stuck with a £380,000 deficit. He'd also heard that Andrew Lloyd Webber had bid £500,000.

I couldn't imagine that *anyone* — especially someone as canny as Andrew, the world's richest, most popular living composer — would announce *any* price before a secret bid, unless he was bluffing. I told Bert Stitt that I'd think about it.

"Well, Ed," he said, "if you *are* interested, think *fast!* All closed bids must be in the hands of the Old Vic trustees no later than June 11."

"When's that?" I asked, without checking.

"About seventy-two hours from now," Bert said.

I thought fast. And hard. And consulted with Anne and David. Then decided. We'd *go* for it!

But since there were only three days left, I didn't want to depend on the mail. So I flew a lawyer over with our offer. I *still* thought Lloyd Webber was bluffing — but I wasn't *sure*.

We bid £550,000.

Exactly two weeks later, on June 23, I got a cable from the trustees — congratulating us on becoming the new owners of the Old Vic Theatre. I was stunned.

It wasn't just the shock and pride of proprietorship, but the discovery that Lloyd Webber had in *fact* bid £500,000. And that famed director Trevor Nunn had also offered a similar figure. For a guy who considered himself pretty shrewd with a deal, I'd overbid them by about a hundred thousand bucks.

When I flew to London to give the trustees their cheque, I discovered that some of the British papers were irate about a foreigner buying their historic landmark. So we called a press conference in the Old Vic auditorium to try and alleviate their concerns. On the way in I overheard a BBC-TV crew ask a man on the street what he thought of a Canuck named Honest Ed owning the Old Vic. "Well, I wouldn't trust *anyone* called Honest," he said. "I'd watch every move he makes." This quote was played across the country.

My reception inside the theatre wasn't much warmer. There were 400 reporters swarming for my blood. But I got up and spoke for ten minutes, then took questions. I explained how, over the years, Sir John and Sir Ralph had made me appreciate the Old Vic's legendary history. I said I didn't feel we *owned* the theatre, because nobody really owns anything. We were only temporary caretakers. What's more, the Old Vic would never move ten feet from where it is. It would not only remain as a theatre, but we intended to totally renovate it as we had the Royal Alex.

HOW
TO
BUILD
AN
EMPIRE
ON AN
ORANGE
CRATE

And finally I said, "They're calling me a foreigner. But I'm really just a lad from the colonies." Thankfully, everyone roared.

After that, the hostility evaporated. But, since the very nature of theatre is 90 per cent talk and 10 per cent reality, there was still considerable scepticism. And it lasted until the press, and finally the public, realized our intentions to restore the theatre were sincere. From that point on, everyone has been incredibly gracious. Yet, to us, the renovations were *essential*. The Old Vic had become a cultural relic of the Industrial Revolution. The *only* thing left of the original building were its four outside walls.

And those were built in 1818 when the theatre was erected on the swamp of Lambeth Marsh. At the time, Lambeth was a quiet rural town on the side of the Thames. But with the construction of the Waterloo Bridge into the area, land speculators poured in, including the three who built the theatre — two previous owners of the Royal Circus and the King's marine painter. After obtaining the royal patronage of the Saxe-Cobourg Prince Leopold, essential for getting a licence, the theatre took two years to complete due to drainage difficulties and near bankruptcy. After one of the trio attempted suicide in debtor's prison, the Waterloo Bridge Company — anxious to encourage traffic through its tollgate — kicked in enough to finish the job and even added streetlights to keep patrons out of the swamp.

By the time it opened as the Royal Cobourg, Lambeth had turned into a teeming industrial slum. To give its usually drunken, always boisterous patrons what they wanted, most shows were violent, action-packed melodramas whose in-house authors stole liberally from the classics. With audiences comprised of factory workers, fish hawkers, thieves, and prostitutes, even added police patrols failed to lure the elite.

Little wonder. As Charles Dickens reported: "At each step up the staircase the warmth and stench increase, until by the time one reaches the gallery doorway, a furnace heat reaches out that seems to force you backwards, whilst the odour positively prevents respiration."

In desperation one owner, Mr. Glossop, installed a costly multi-ton "Looking Glass Curtain" for his 1821 Boxing Day premiere of *The Temple of Death*. Widely advertised, the curtain did attract many who loved to watch their own reflections. But after three years the novelty had worn off and it was dismantled. A series of new managers took over, and most made major alterations to attract new audiences—who, if they came, soon fled. Those foolish enough to buy expensive pit seats soon discovered the gallery's delight in pouring beer upon them from above.

Yet by 1843 major changes had been made. The theatre was called the Royal Victoria (after the princess who'd been enticed to attend and never came again). Shakespeare and adaptations of Dickens were presented, and while seating had been increased to 1,500, often more than 2,000 patrons packed the place. Although gas lighting had replaced candles, it was still a firetrap—as

HOW
TO
BUILD
AN
EMPIRE
ON AN
ORANGE
CRATE

evidenced one night in 1858 when someone falsely shouted "Fire!" and among the sixty-five trampled in the instant stampede, sixteen died.

By 1870, while still Georgian outside, the interior was entirely Victorian, yet both exterior and interior were in disrepair. After plans to wreck it for a music hall failed, the place was entirely refurbished except for the walls and roof. Yet by then a sprawling outdoor market surrounded the theatre, and the district was one of London's worst. Though the theatre was twice put up for auction in the decade, its doors were shut in 1880.

It was Emma Cons who saved it. A forty-five-year-old temperance reformer who hated the music hall "booze palaces" and believed that "to keep men happy keeps men good", Emma was inspired to rent the Old Vic for £1,000 a year in the name of the "Coffee Palace Association". Reopening the theatre on Boxing Day 1880, she instantly banned alcohol, whores, bawdy plays, and musicals, replacing them with coffee, concerts, temperance lectures, gymnasium and games room, magic-lantern shows, and Sunday services.

News of Emma's good works swiftly spread. In 1891, having raised £17,000 in less than four months, she bought the theatre's freehold in the name of the Royal Victoria Hall Foundation, which managed it for the next ninety-four years. Then she built a school, Morley College, behind, above, and below the stage. Even without audiences, the theatre was jammed.

In 1898, with Emma's health failing, she was joined

by her twenty-three-year-old niece, Lilian Baylis, who had just left her family's touring musical act in South Africa. Lilian agreed to help manage the theatre for one year. She helped out for forty. By the time Emma died in 1912, Lilian Baylis was in total command. After Morley College's 1,800 students were ousted at the end of World War I, Lilian devoted her entire life to the Old Vic, becoming the most important theatre manager London ever had.

She not only introduced operas and ballet to its stage, but, under such inspired directors as Tyrone Guthrie, brought back Shakespeare. Soon, even though Old Vic wages were infinitely less than those in the West End, actors were knocking at her door. They included almost all of the future acting Lords (Wolfit, Olivier, Richardson, Redgrave, Gielgud, Guinness) and Ladies (Evans, Robson, Ashcroft, Thorndike, Maggie Smith)—and some, like Laughton, Elsa Lanchester, and Vivien Leigh, who should have been.

A total eccentric and devout Catholic who talked to God constantly (asking for more money and cheaper actors) Lilian often cooked sausages backstage (sending the aroma drifting over audiences), loudly told Queen Mary who arrived late for a matinee, "I'm glad you've turned up at last, dear, but we've got a long programme, so let's get on with it," and scolded her entire company for racing to an air-raid shelter during the Blitz, "If you have to be killed, at least die at your job."

HOW
TO
BUILD
AN
EMPIRE
ON AN
ORANGE
CRATE

Finally, after turning the Old Vic into the Holy Grail of Shakespearean drama, Baylis died in 1937—just four years before her beloved theatre was *indeed* hit by a bomb and shut. Guthrie toured the company outside war-ravaged London until the theatre reopened in 1950. But in 1963, the famous Old Vic Company was disbanded—to provide a thirteen-year tenure by the government-backed National Theatre directed by the great Sir Larry—then resurrected in 1978 for triumphal tours of Britain and the Continent.

Yet in 1981, when government subsidies suddenly stopped, the Old Vic's governors were stuck with a £380,000 deficit and had to sell. So the following year, that's where I came in. And, after 174 years of hard-drinking rabble, reflecting curtains, false fire disasters, tub-thumping teetotalers, constant alterations, buzz bombs, and Peter O'Toole, the poor old theatre was pretty dilapidated. It cost us over $1 million to buy it. But its total restoration cost $3.9 million more.

To begin with, I went through the theatre with Anne and the theatre administrator, Andrew Leigh, and listed all the criteria for its restoration. After seven architectural firms submitted plans on how they'd deal with these criteria and solve the problems, we selected the London firm RWHL for the job. Then we took the most beautiful period of the Old Vic's architectural history, which was 1881, and restored the auditorium to that time.

The only thing I insisted on was that the warren of small committee offices covering the entire front end of the building be cleared out, and the space returned to the public in lobbies and lounge bars. And the architects and designers did a spectacular job.

Today the auditorium, with its forty-foot-high, pewter-grey and coral ceiling dominated by a massive chandelier, is a blend of plush velvet seats and ornately moulded balcony façades evoking a long-past era. Three pairs of boxes draped in burgundy velvet are stacked on each side of the stage. The walls are covered in dark grey Victorian-style wallpaper, and the balconies are tinted in silver, cream, and gold.

During the renovations, we hung a giant banner from the scaffolding on Waterloo Road that read: "Lilian Baylis, you're going to love this. Honest Ed." And when they were completed, we took out ads in the trade journals to thank the British workers who'd finished the job on schedule. Then, for the gala reopening on October 31, 1983, we dazzled the audience with airport runway lights down the entire length of Waterloo Road and beamed searchlights from the entrance.

The honoured guest that evening was the Royal Patron of the Old Vic in person—Her Majesty Queen Elizabeth, the Queen Mother. Anne, David, and his lovely wife, Audrey, joined me in greeting her, and I tried to be on my best behaviour.

This was because at a dinner a few nights before, I'd turned to Prince Charles and said, "Your granny's going to open our theatre this week," and Anne had kicked me under the table.

HOW
TO
BUILD
AN
EMPIRE
ON AN
ORANGE
CRATE

So on opening night I was especially good—even though it's been reported that during an exchange of introductions I said to a member of the royal entourage, "Hi, I'm Honest Ed."

It absolutely isn't true. Shortly after we acquired the theatre, the Queen Mum graciously invited us to Clarence House for a reception. *That* was the night I said it.

CHAPTER THIRTEEN

In 1989 Anne and I went to Russia as guests of the Gorbachev government.

While touring the famous Hermitage in Leningrad, we were told one section of the building was reserved for artisans skilled in the restoration of old buildings. Then a few days later we were in the magnificent Odessa Opera House, and both fell in love with it.

Back in Moscow I told a top-ranking official at a reception, "You know, down the street from our theatre in Toronto we've got this empty parking lot. If you can arrange for those craftsmen from the Hermitage to come over and build an exact replica of the Odessa Opera House in our lot, I'll pay all the labour costs in hard currency. This could be a monument to Canadian-USSR friendship."

When the word was passed on to the appropriate department, the Russians were wildly excited about the

HOW
TO
BUILD
AN
EMPIRE
ON AN
ORANGE
CRATE

idea. And I was delighted as well, for the Odessa Opera House has six tiers of boxes. A total of 140 separate boxes. And I figured if I could sell one box to 140 different corporations, it would pay for the construction.

After returning to Canada, we kept in close touch with the Russians. Then they started sending over plans, and people to check the site. They were still excited about the project—but we could never break it down. The wheels of Soviet bureaucracy ground sluggishly. The procrastinating went on for ages. Then suddenly the USSR collapsed. And thus ended—at least temporarily—the plans for Odessa Opera House II.

Meanwhile Cameron Mackintosh was electrifying London with his musical bombshell, *Miss Saigon*, which had opened with the largest advance sale in West End history. We'd been friends ever since he brought his first production, *Relatively Speaking*, to the Royal Alexandra sixteen years before. And we'd worked together on numerous shows in the interim. On one trip to London I told Cameron we'd like to co-produce *Miss Saigon* in the Alex, but he said the stage was far too small.

That's when I thought of the parking lot again. With *Miss Saigon* building into the biggest theatrical hit of all time, I thought we could build a temporary theatre in the lot to produce it alone. Then, when the show finally ended its run, we could tear the place down. The idea died when I found, first of all, that *Miss Saigon* was costing $10 million, back then, just to *mount*.

And also, by simply looking around, I had the feeling

that the fastest-growing trend in theatre was *bigness*! Shows like *Cats*, *Les Miz*, and *Phantom of the Opera* were also breaking records. The top stage producers of the nineties were selling vastly expensive yet hugely *visual* presentations, which the public was buying like mad. There was obviously a market there for big costly productions.

And, of course, they needed big stages. So David and I decided to go ahead and build a theatre on the parking lot for *Miss Saigon*. But it wouldn't be temporary. It would have one of North America's largest stages, and the finest technical facilities of any theatre in the world. We hired award-winning architect Peter Smith as the theatre's designer, and Glenn Pushelberg and George Yabu for interior design.

We yanked down all those huge electric signs proclaiming "Ed's World Famous Restaurants" and their giant steel supports, and closed the parking lot gate for the last time on August 5, 1991. The following morning 400 guests arrived to find the guard's booth gone, and Toronto Mayor Art Eggleton greeting them instead. Beside him stood a shorter chap no one seemed to know.

Then a giant backhoe in the corner roared to life, its shovel high in the air, and rumbled to the centre of the lot. Its massive scoop came swinging down as if to gobble a huge chunk of asphalt—and David and I stepped out of it in white coveralls and hard hats. When the crowd cheered I raised a hand and said, "You ain't seen nothin' yet."

HOW
TO
BUILD
AN
EMPIRE
ON AN
ORANGE
CRATE

We got on a stage in the corner with the mayor and his companion, and I introduced Cameron Mackintosh —the man who'd produced 250 productions around the world in the past twenty years, including the biggest hit musical in history. Then we pointed to the wall of our Lewiscraft building on the east side of the lot—and up rose a five-storey-high red silk banner announcing the coming of *Miss Saigon* and the new theatre being built to stage it. We told the crowd it would be the first legitimate theatre built in North America since the O'Keefe Centre was erected in Toronto three decades before—*and* the first to be funded by private money since the Royal Alex was built in 1905. Everyone cheered like crazy.

We said it would have 2,000 seats—500 more than the Alex—on the horseshoe-shaped orchestra floor— and two balconies. Elevators would whisk patrons to the lobby from four underground parking levels. Frank Stella, one of the world's pre-eminent abstract artists, would create eighteen original murals for the lobby. He would also paint the dome of the auditorium, the proscenium arch of the stage, and a huge exterior mural on the the- atre's eight-storey fly tower. The world's hottest musical would be staged in the world's most modern setting. Applause resounded through the lot.

Then David, Cameron, the mayor, and I each took a gold-plated shovel and dug the first holes of the founda- tion. That was the start of it.

The theatre cost $50 million to erect. That includes the $23 million construction cost, the $20 million value of the land—plus $7 million in additional parking space.

To stage *Miss Saigon* itself cost another $12 million—by far the greatest amount ever spent on a show in Canada. (It's as much as *Les Misérables* and *Phantom of the Opera* combined.) David and I co-produce it with Cameron Mackintosh. Yet we figured from the beginning that the costs would be recouped within the first year if it sells out completely. And both the show *and* the theatre would be paid for the *second* year if it sells 80 per cent of the seats.

We're hopeful. By opening night, the box office had already rung up $30 million in advance ticket sales—the biggest advance sale in Canadian history. And those were only seats for the first seven months. When the show is finally over, however, *Miss Saigon*'s gift to Toronto will be one of the finest 2,000-seat theatres in the world. We're certain it will run long enough to justify us taking the risk.

Ever since the theatre was announced, the media had been speculating about its name. Would it be called "The Mirvish", "Ed's Palace", or what? In truth, we didn't know. But two factors led to our final decision. The finest theatre in Toronto until the Royal Alex went up was the Princess, just a block away on King, which was built in 1889 —and demolished in 1931. By using the name "Princess" we were not only paying homage to a historical Toronto theatre, but keeping to the same regal tradition as the Royal Alexandra and the Royal Victoria (or Old Vic).

HOW
TO
BUILD
AN
EMPIRE
ON AN
ORANGE
CRATE

And because the entire Mirvish family had great admiration for Diana, Princess of Wales—both for her tireless work with children, the elderly, and the ailing, and because we'd delighted in her company when she joined us at the Royal Alex in 1991 to see *Les Misérables*— her title seemed highly appropriate. And so when we received a letter from Kensington Palace in January 1993, saying "I am delighted to have the opportunity to contribute to the continuation of two theatrical traditions," with the signature, "Diana", the name, as we announced, was finally official.

It would be called "The Princess of Wales Theatre".

Besides the name, its official opening, May 14, 1993, was also appropriate. It was exactly ten years since our ownership and restoration of the Old Vic, and exactly thirty years since we'd restored and reopened the Royal Alexandra.

The opening night was spectacular. Taxis, limousines, cars, and hand-pulled rickshaws stalled traffic around the theatre as they nosed towards the entrance to disgorge our 2,000 guests beneath the searchlights. Before the curtain the audience rose to salute Governor General Ray Hnatyshyn, the Queen's representative in Canada; he and his wife, Gerda, were the guests of honour in our box. Among the other dignitaries were Ontario Premier Bob Rae, former lieutenant-governor Lincoln Alexander, Mayor June Rowlands, Metro Chairman Alan Tonks, and most of the city's top politicians.

At the thunderous curtain call there was a standing

ovation for the cast before producer Cameron Mackintosh and *Miss Saigon*'s creators, Alain Boubil and Claude-Michel Schonberg, joined David and me on stage. And then the party started.

It was held in a giant warehouse at the foot of Jarvis Street, and traffic was again jammed through downtown streets for nearly ninety minutes. The huge Marine Warehouse had been abandoned for four years except for pigeons. But New York designer Jim McNabb collaborated with Toronto's Jeffry Royck to turn the place into a palace.

After laying 40,000 square feet of carpeting and nearly 2 miles of electric cables for lights, and covering the walls with 11,000 feet of pitch-black draping made of parachute material, they then covered all tables and 2,000 chairs with ivory muslin, brought in 800 palm trees, 20,000 pieces of china, 30 chefs, Guido Basso's 14-piece orchestra, and 130 staff, while, within the entrance hall, they dangled an actual helicopter from the ceiling. It took 3 months of planning, plus 180 workers and 6 days just to set it up. The effect was sensational.

Guests included journalists from Australia to England, stage producers from Germany to Japan, prima ballerinas Veronica Tennant and Karen Kain, *Saturday Night Live* producer Lorne Michaels, film directors David Cronenberg and Harry Rasky, singers Michael Burgess, Salome Bey, and Catherine McKinnon, comedians Frank Shuster and Don Harron, performers Al Waxman, Jan Rubes, Dinah Christie, and Tom Kneebone, as well as Sonia Bata and Jane Jacobs.

HOW
TO
BUILD
AN
EMPIRE
ON AN
ORANGE
CRATE

Throughout the night the crowd went through 1,000 kilos of Vietnamese-style chicken, poached salmon, and beef, plus 8,000 hors d'oeuvres. They sailed on the three-masted *Empire Sandy*, which docked at the lakeside door, and quaffed champagne steadily till 5 A.M., when breakfast was served for the last remaining guests. It was, many said, the best big party they'd ever been at.

We thought so, too. It was quite a week. A few days before I'd been named Toronto's first "Ambassador", and a few days later I was given the Beth Sholom Brotherhood's prestigious Humanitarian Award for "splendid achievement in the field of human service".

But the highlight, of course, was the opening of the Princess of Wales Theatre. Three decades before, we'd bought the Royal Alex because I thought it was a bargain. It finally seemed obvious we were in the theatre business for keeps.

Some people say we've built an empire on an orange crate. But looking back, I now realize that from the time I started working in that grocery store on Dundas Street, it's taken seventy years to become an overnight success.

ED'S LESSONS FROM LIFE

1.

I've tried by example to show my son the merits of hard work. In return he taught me not to brag about it.

When David was young, I told him once how I'd toiled as a kid to get ahead. I went on for minutes, building up to the punch line, which I knew for sure would slay him: "In fact," said I, "I started working when I was *nine*."

David looked up, his eyes wide with wonderment. "But what were you before *that*, Daddy?" he asked. "A bum?"

From the mouth of a babe, but I've never forgotten.

If you think you're so terrific, let someone else boast about it. No one wants to hear it from you.

HOW
TO
BUILD
AN
EMPIRE
ON AN
ORANGE
CRATE

2.

Although with just nine years of schooling I've achieved some success it doesn't mean I'm against a formal education. Just the opposite. When I had to drop out of Central Tech at fifteen, I felt I'd been cheated out of something I was *entitled* to. I've always believed proper schooling provides you with an invaluable tool kit to carry into a career. I know I'd have learned far more if I'd finished. But I didn't have the chance.

Most of my education I got in the streets. And, looking back, it was *some* education. But still, I often wonder whether, if I'd gone through school, I would be where I am today. Truthfully, I doubt it. I've concluded there are two types of learning:

Schooling's what you get in the schoolroom. Education's what you get in the poolroom.

3.

On Dundas Street, where I grew up, almost every barber was a bookie. Every single day the neighbourhood gamblers, hustlers, hucksters, thieves, bootleggers, sharpies, panhandlers, pimps, and pool sharks sashayed through the doors beneath the striped poles to place horserace bets with the barbers. The bets, of course, were illegal. Gambling is legal only when the government gets a cut.

Usually, when the betters hit the barbershops, they stayed. The barbershops on Dundas Street were very crowded joints. And between taking bets, some barbers even barbered. There was always a long queue. So whenever I went for a haircut in Magner's barber shop across the street, I *knew* I'd *always* be last in line. I expected it. As the squirt in Mirvish's grocery store, I hardly headed the pecking order.

But I never minded the wait. It meant I didn't have to work for an hour or so. And besides, I was getting a free, and incredibly widespread, education. All I had to do was sit. And listen. And learn.

Even when my turn for a cut *did* come up, I knew I'd still be put on hold if any local high-roller was in a rush. They'd tap dance in, wafting a buck, and say, "Hey, Mag, old buddy, I need a fast shave." And I'd sit. And wait.

So I couldn't believe it one day I went in. The joint was jammed, so I sat in a corner, prepared for my usual holding pattern. Then suddenly a guy darted in from the street and whispered in the barber's ear. Magner frantically looked around . . . and saw *me*! "YOU, Eddie," he shouted. "*Get* in the chair."

I was totally baffled. "But it's not my turn," I protested. "I just walked in. It's *not* my. . . ."

"Shut UP," he screamed. "It IS your turn. Just get in the damn chair NOW!"

I weaved across the room. The barber threw down some papers, yanked me up by my belt into the chair, and whipped a sheet around me in a second flat. "But, Mr. Magner," I kept peeping, "it isn't my turn." In the mirror I

HOW
TO
BUILD
AN
EMPIRE
ON AN
ORANGE
CRATE

saw every face in the room glaring at me. And like a Greek chorus, the gamblers hissed in unison, "Yes, it *IS*."

I couldn't believe it. Then, the instant Magner's scissors started clicking, three detectives charged in.

For forty minutes they searched the shop for the betting slips. The barber grumbled, but kept cutting. The cops pulled out drawers and frisked the customers. Finally, in silent fury, they left.

"All right, Eddie," said Magner, snapping off the sheet, "you're done." Then he scooped up the pile of slips I'd been sitting on. "Thanks, son," he said, and patted my head. The gamblers almost applauded.

It was the only time I ever got instant service in that shop. But besides the reminder that we don't always live in a legal society, I learned two important things that day.

When the other guy's bigger and stronger, it's dumb to keep arguing. It's smarter to back off and stay in the game, so you'll know what to do the next time.

But the greatest lesson was this: **If you have something that someone else needs, you can get immediate service.**

4.

Bootleggers were as common as the bookies in our district, but they ran their operations in private homes on side streets. Besides selling booze in bottles, they poured whiskey by the glass in their parlours. And the vast majority of their patrons were not the neighbour-hood immigrants (who could barely afford milk), but the long-standing, upright citizens who ran the city. Judges, doctors, developers, businessmen, lawyers, even aldermen.

One bootlegger once bragged to me, "I always do business with the very best people. Some of the biggest men in Toronto drink at *my* joint." He told me some of their names. They were *big*.

Bootlegging, like book-making, was, of course, illegal. But no one around Dundas considered them crimes. They were more like *careers*. Most bookies and booze merchants were family men trying to make a buck in a new land. They'd picked their professions because they were in demand. And the majority were honest men. They settled winning bets promptly, slaked appreciative thirsts with sizeable shots, and invariably paid local merchants, like my parents, in cash. But the authorities considered them crooks. They were breaking the law. And almost every night the streets shrilled with whistles as the cops made raids.

Times have changed. Today politicians not only encourage gambling, but organize it themselves through million-dollar lotteries. And they not only permit sales of alcohol, but push it themselves through provincial liquor stores. None is privately owned, as you know.

On the street as a kid I often heard the line, "If you can't do the time, don't do the crime." Yet most crimes of that time no longer exist. I've finally figured it out.

HOW
TO
BUILD
AN
EMPIRE
ON AN
ORANGE
CRATE

Vices become virtues overnight if governments can profit from them.

5.

The social life of our neighbourhood was the neighbourhood itself. Besides the cinema and different delis, for those who could afford them, most socializing took place in the synagogue and little family stores. People thrived on the local gossip, and the shopkeepers heard it all. A woman would pop in for a tin of beans and leave—loaded with juicy news—an hour later. Our entire world centred on the Dundas Street strip. People were poor but generally content, because so many had come from unhappier lands.

The advent of radio was like a miracle. We'd cluster around our crystal sets agog. Then, when television arrived, it opened up the world. But these new wonders also brought discontent. The kids I knew began to imagine that some big party was going on out there—and they hadn't been invited. The feeling was that we were being cheated.

I've seen the world and the big party since. I've even been to Buckingham Palace. But I look back at that time on Dundas Street when our world, a few blocks long, was so small. So naïvely, provincially, exuberantly cloistered. And happy.

And I realize now:

What you don't know, you don't miss.

6.

Our grocery store on Dundas Street was always broke. We constantly gave credit, and most customers didn't pay. Not because they were dishonest, but because they were always broke too. For me to deliver groceries at midnight, then not get paid for them, didn't seem to make sense. Long before I went into business I realized:

It doesn't take a genius to know it's stupid to work for no reward. And it's even dumber to sell something for nothing.

That's why, when I opened Honest Ed's, all sales were strictly for cash.

7.

I was poor as a kid. Now I'm not. I was lucky as a kid. I'm lucky now. I've been lucky all my life.

Even as a kid I knew that my parents, my relatives, and most of our neighbours had left homes in Europe, suffered extreme hardships, made sacrifices, and even faced death before fleeing to a land of freedom. I knew how fortunate, how privileged, I was to be born in it. I'd been handed opportunity on a platter, and I was lucky to have the common sense to recognize it—and go after it. Still, no matter what I've done, I know:

No amount of hard work and brains can beat plain dumb luck.

HOW
TO
BUILD
AN
EMPIRE
ON AN
ORANGE
CRATE

8.

As a teenager, I'd often drift down to Queen's Park to listen to the fiery orations of Tim Buck, Joseph Salzberg, and Sam Carr, the leaders of Canada's Communist Party and trade unions, and marvel at how they could speak with such passion and conviction for an hour without a single note. Since my father had filled me in on communism's crimes, I listened as a sceptic. But still, the fervour of these men amazed me, and they taught me something I've always remembered:

To sell your beliefs with true conviction, you must truly believe what you say.

9.

When my father ran our store on Dundas, the top shelves were usually empty. After he died, the first thing I did was to stack all those shelves with empty cans and boxes. It didn't matter they were dummies. They made it look like we had lots to sell. They made the store look more *prosperous*.

After that, I changed all the light bulbs to 200 watts to illuminate the entire room, for I'd noticed two things in the big department stores and supermarkets:

Bright lights lure customers like moths.

And: **The bigger the display of merchandise, the more people buy.**

That's why Honest Ed's has the biggest electric store

sign in the world with 23,000 constantly flashing light bulbs, and our hydro bill is $10,000 a month.

It's also why most of our merchandise is heaped in humongous piles.

10.

Putting "Honest" in front of your name takes nerve; most people instantly assume that you're *not*. Among them are three rabbis I know who think anyone named "Honest" needs serious help.

One keeps asking me to study the Talmud with him one morning each week. I tried it once and admit it was probably good for my soul. After the study, the rabbi served a slice of his wife's apple strudel. It was scrumptious. I'm ashamed to say that the strudel was the main thing that tempted me to return—but my schedule has always interfered.

Still, the good rabbi hasn't given up on old "Honest". He still calls once a week, beseeching me to return. I'd like to, I say, but I'm just so darn busy. He always sighs and says, "Ah, Yehuda [he never calls me Ed], Yehuda. Some day you're going to have to meet your maker. When that day comes, you will not be ready. All these things you say are keeping you so busy can't help you one bit on the Judgement Day. You won't have the answers."

Once, I told him, "Rabbi, for years I've dealt with suppliers for our store and restaurants. I've dealt with New York and London producers for our theatres. They're

115

HOW
TO
BUILD
AN
EMPIRE
ON AN
ORANGE
CRATE

some of the toughest guys you could ever deal with. Surely, if I can work out a deal with them, rabbi, I should have no trouble with God who is all understanding and compassionate."

There was a second of silence, then the rabbi yelled, "DON'T GET SMART, Yehuda."

What did I learn from this?

Don't get too smart! Especially with people who have strong opinions.

11.

Although my family wasn't deeply religious, we did have a kosher home, and my father always took us to High Holidays at the synagogue. When he died we had prayers every morning and evening for eleven months in mourning. Then later, the synagogue split into Conservative and Orthodox congregations. I didn't know which one to go to so I joined both. Then when I got married, it was in the Reformed Temple in Hamilton because Anne sang in the choir. So we joined the Holy Blossom in Toronto, and now I belong to all three congregations. You can't, I figure, be *too* safe.

The president of one of the synagogues phoned me one day. "Congratulations, Ed," he said, "you got lucky."

"I'm *already* lucky," I said.

"Just *listen*, will ya! You just won a *raffle*."

"That's nice," I said. "What did I win?"

"A Torah," he shouted. "You won a T*orah*!"

Torahs, as you know, are huge religious scrolls inscribed with Hebrew prayers which are kept in a synagogue's sanctuary.

"I don't remember buying any raffle ticket," I told him. "And besides, what could I possibly do with a Torah?"

"Well," said the president, "you could donate it to a synagogue in Israel."

"I could," I agreed, "and it sounds like a splendid idea. So donate it to a synagogue in Israel, okay?" Then I said, "Sorry, but I really gotta run."

"Hey, *wait*, Ed." He sounded frantic. "It's not that simple. It will cost five hundred dollars to pack it, insure it, and ship it."

And what was the lesson from that? **You get nothing but nothing for nothing, other than added expense.**

12.

Outside my office in Honest Ed's is the sprawling shoe department. Piles of cheap sneakers and sandals are heaped on stands just beyond the door. Because we're strictly a self-service store, the shoes are tied together in pairs. (Imagine the mess if they weren't.) To avoid the chaos of separated footwear, I put big signs through the whole section stating: "It Is Illegal To Separate Shoes".

Then one day a lady stopped me and jabbed a finger at the sign. "Tell me, Mr. Mirvish," she demanded, "who passed this stupid law . . . and *why*? Does it mean I gotta walk around like this the rest of my life?"

HOW
TO
BUILD
AN
EMPIRE
ON AN
ORANGE
CRATE

I looked down, and her shoes were linked together with long laces.

The lesson? *If you make the rules, they had better make sense. And if you can't enforce them, don't make them.*

13.

Years ago when our store was much smaller, we had one narrow staircase connecting all four floors. But shoppers incessantly complained about the constant shoving and congestion. And I always listen to my customers.

So when we expanded, with a huge new addition, I insisted two broad new stairways be installed. Thus, thought I, ends the problem.

I thought wrong. And it baffles me still. Even on our busiest days, when the store makes a beehive seem spacious, the broader stairways are rarely used. The mobs still jam the narrow old staircase. And *still* complain how crammed it is.

There's only one thing I can figure from this: **People would sooner suffer than change old habits.**

Either that or: **What people say and what they do would provide Sigmund Freud with six books.**

14.

I've learned through the years to run a smart business, but I've never claimed to be brilliant. Even though I try to anticipate customer wants, they never fail to surprise me. Like the guy who stopped me on the street and said, "I just staggered out of your store, Ed. Jeez was it crowded. Women crushing me on one side, shoving on the other. I could barely move."

I'd heard it before and knew what was coming: he'd *never* set foot in the store again. I put out my hand to apologize, and he grabbed it. "It sure was nice, Ed. I really enjoyed it. I'm going back tomorrow and let those ladies squeeze me again."

The man proved again what I should have known: **Pleasures come from strange places, so don't close any doors.**

15.

As Robin Leach once brayed on his TV show, "Honest Ed will do *anything* to grab your attention—and money." He's absolutely right. I'll even appear on "Lifestyles of the Rich and Famous". Although privately I'm basically low key, I've tried to be as flamboyant as I can because in business it attracts attention. And I'm shameless when it comes to getting free advertising. It makes sense.

The best publicity doesn't cost you a cent.
It is merchandising in its simplest form.

16.

One of our most widely ballyhooed promotions was "Honest Ed's Win-A-Date-With-A-Star" contest on

HOW
TO
BUILD
AN
EMPIRE
ON AN
ORANGE
CRATE

Victoria Day, 1958. This was the major draw of our *Dream Holiday Sale* in which, for the first time, we opened on an official holiday. Bob Gray dreamed up the "Dreams", which included a private Georgian Bay island for $2.19, a luxury boat cruise for two for $1.99, a swimming pool for 88 cents, a weekend for two in Manhattan for $2.19, and—the biggest dream of all—a deluxe dinner date with a star for 79 cents.

All anyone had to do to win a dream sale was stand on some secret spot in the store at a specific time. The papers thought it was crazy, but naturally played it up. And 27,000 customers elbowed in that day—most wearing big, broad shoes. As the ads had promised, one female winner would get to date actor-singer Robert Goulet, and some lucky male would get a date with actress Toby Robins. There was just one hitch: Bob Gray had forgotten to tell Toby.

Two days before the Dream Sale, Miss Robins appeared at the store in person. To be accurate, she shot through the door like a Texas tornado. She whipped out a copy of the newspaper ad. She wafted it in the faces of staff and startled customers. She tore it into tiny shreds. She yanked a Dream Date display sign out of a window. She ripped the sign up too. She wasn't one bit happy.

I didn't blame her one bit either.

But since, as it seemed, Toby didn't *want* to be a dream date, Lorraine Messinger found a replacement in singer-actress Margot MacKinnon (whom, I made sure, had been *told*). And the Dream Dates were held. A nineteen-year-old Ontario Hydro typist, Joyce Hegin-bottom (who'd come in to buy paint), won the 79-cent date with Goulet. A thirteen-year-old Runnymede High School student, David Webb (who'd wandered in to buy film), won the date with MacKinnon. The store dressed them both in fine apparel—then whisked them by limo to the Royal York Hotel's posh Imperial Room for their elegant double date.

There was just one other hitch. Bob Gray had forgotten to reserve the quartet a table. And the room was packed. As photographers buzzed around waiting for photos, and Bob disappeared to the bar, Lorraine Messinger convinced the maître d' (with a profitable handshake) to set up a spare table. The Dream Date was saved. She'd done it again. Another lesson learned.

If you can't be there to mend a mistake, make sure you've got someone who CAN.

17.

I was just recovering from this latest near fiasco when I got a call from the winner of the $2.19 island in Georgian Bay. It turned out the deed required him to build on the island within twelve months or forfeit it. And he didn't even have enough money to build a doghouse. He'd barely had the $2.19 to buy the *property*. He wasn't one bit happy. I didn't blame *him*, either. So I bought back the island, which I've *still* never seen, for a few hundred more than $2.19. And that *did* make him happy, I'm happy to say.

HOW
TO
BUILD
AN
EMPIRE
ON AN
ORANGE
CRATE

But still, with the luck I was having with Bob's schemes, I worried for weeks. Every day I expected a phone call informing me that the $1.99 New York week-end couple had been mugged, the $1.99 cruise liner had run aground, and the 88-cent swimming pool had sunk with all hands.

The promotion, as usual, got us piles of free print. But regarding Miss Robins, free islands, and table reservations, it had been a disaster. I learned—as I *should* have from all Bob Gray's stunts:

Before you jump into anything BIG always check the DETAILS first.

18.

For years I've had this dream: To build a canal down Markham Street—all the way from Mirvish Village to Lake Ontario. I'd arch bridges across it, float gondolas up and down it, put footpaths and cafés alongside it. In winter you could skate on it, in summer you could swim.

I think it's a glorious idea. Canals are tranquil, beautiful creations—and incredible tourist attractions. Look at Venice. San Antonio. Amsterdam.

As for Toronto, it has one of the best big city administrations anywhere. But when I approached it with my plan, Toronto City Council turned it down. And the lesson I learned was this:

It may be good, but it can always be better.

19

I have never taken a business course. Therefore, I've always tried to avoid complicated "service" systems. Honest Ed's, for instance, has no "sales clerks" per se. Most employees you see in the store stock supplies. I like to keep things simple.

For instance, we opened Ed's Warehouse after buying the Royal Alex, only because we hoped they would complement each other. And, because I knew zilch about the restaurant business and wanted to keep it simple, we decided to serve only one item. I'd heard that some restaurants, like Lowry's in Los Angeles and Simpson's in London, had become famous serving roast beef. What's more, you didn't need a genius master chef to prepare it, and it was simple to serve. So that's what we settled on. Good Old-Fashioned English *Roast Beef*—even though I never much liked it, and still don't.

When I told them what we planned, veteran restaurateurs were shocked. They had already told me I was nuts to even contemplate a restaurant. But the thought of a single-entrée menu was insane. People can't eat roast beef *every* night, they said. And besides, on Fridays, Catholics can't eat it *at all*.

"Who says so?" I asked.

"The Pope," they told me.

I listened to all the arguments, then made my decision. We served *only* roast beef. Then, right after we opened (although I'm sure it was sheer coincidence), the Pope

HOW
TO
BUILD
AN
EMPIRE
ON AN
ORANGE
CRATE

changed the rules: people *could* eat meat on Fridays. The place has been packed ever since. The moral I think is obvious.

Listen to your instincts and follow your convictions.

20.

Two of the most regular patrons of Ed's Warehouse when it opened were Mayor Nathan Phillips and his wife. The restaurant had been running for nearly two years when we realized that Mrs. Phillips always asked the waiter to leave the bone on her cut of beef. Until then, we'd been tossing all the bones into the garbage. (I told you I knew *nothing* about cuisine.)

It finally dawned on me that if dem bones were good enough for the mayor's wife, other diners might like them too. So the following day we started barbecuing the bones. Since then, from our own supply of prime rib, we've sold *every single one.*

I once worked it out. In the first two years we threw out $65,000 worth of bones. That's ten times more than my father *earned* in his lifetime—let alone what he gave in *credit.*

The very memory still gives me heartburn. But thinking of the tons of barbecued ribs we've sold in the decades since eases the pain incredibly.

Of course, one moral of the story is: **You get the mayor you elect, but it helps far more if his spouse is smart.**

The other is obvious: **You don't have to be a chemist to turn garbage into money.**

21.

The first two chefs I hired for Ed's Warehouse were Italian and Portuguese. Their nationalities didn't make any difference. Whenever I walked into the kitchen to suggest anything, they'd *both* chase me out with cleavers.

What in the devil's name, they screamed, did *I* know about cooking?

"Nothing," I admitted, "but I *do* know how to attract customers." To say they were unimpressed is an understatement.

So I called in a smart seventeen-year-old Italian kid who'd once worked in my plastic factory and was then running Honest Ed's parking lot. "Tony," I said, "I want you to work in the kitchen for a while and watch the chefs when they cook the roast beef. If you think you can do it yourself, come and tell me."

Three weeks later he came back and said, "Mr. Mirvish, there's nothing to it. You just shove the beef in the oven and let it cook slowly in its own juice."

So I fired the two professional chefs and put young Tony Fallico in charge of the kitchen. He's been running all 2,600 seats in our restaurants for the past 30 years.

All the experts in the world can't beat good common sense.

HOW
TO
BUILD
AN
EMPIRE
ON AN
ORANGE
CRATE

22.

Soon after we opened Ed's Warehouse, a famous roast-beef restaurateur from Los Angeles visited us and said they always covered their beef with rock salt while it was roasting in the oven. Since the man was considered a master, that's what we did.

But after Tony took over he told me the prime ribs of beef are covered with a fat cap which he felt that neither rock salt nor anything else would penetrate. So he asked if I'd let him try it *without* the salt, since he didn't think it would make a bit of difference. And it *didn't*—to the meat.

Where it *did* make a difference was a tremendous saving in the tons of rock salt we'd previously purchased, plus hours of labour each day to clean it from the ovens. We haven't used rock salt in three decades. Once again I'd discovered:

Traditional methods aren't always the best. Improvisation often pays off.

23.

I'd already learned that lesson at the store, as well as with the interior designer who wanted to tear down all the pillars in Ed's Warehouse—at the cost of $5,000 each. In retrospect, it would have been disastrous. Besides adding character to the room, the tall columns provided a place to hang the hundreds of 8-by-10 photos of stage stars in our collection—as *well* as a place to hang customers' coats. Thus saving the cost and confusion of a cloak room.

This was the same guy who recommended chairs at sixty-five dollars each. After I'd fired him and filled the restaurant with the five-buck second-hand chairs from Crippled Civilians and the Sally Ann, *everyone* told me how *cosy* they were. They didn't match any more than the dishes did, but they *felt* good.

In fact, I told customers if they *liked* the chairs so much, they could *buy* the ones they were sitting on. And some of them actually did!

If it's comfortable, forget about artistic correctness.

24.

Besides the chairs, I also told diners they could buy any antiques in the restaurant at bargain rates as well. But these offers didn't last too long when the value of the items started soaring. The Tiffany-style lamps and hanging lampshades, for instance — of which I'd bought 600 for as little as twenty-five dollars — were suddenly in demand by collectors. (Today, even reproductions are hugely expensive.) And finally the chairs were suffering from the punishment of heavy traffic.

So at last I went to the War Assets Sales and bought 3,000 office chairs (for another $5 each), which are still in the restaurants today. My reason for buying them was first, if a clerk could sit in them eight hours a day, they *had* to be comfortable. And second, they had arms. I'd noticed that

HOW
TO
BUILD
AN
EMPIRE
ON AN
ORANGE
CRATE

diners in fancy chairs *without* arms inevitably wind up with their elbows on the table. Which means they're not easy in their seats. The point seems obvious:

Always keep the customers relaxed. They are far more likely to come back.

25.

When Ed's Warehouse first opened I had a friend in the laundry business who supplied us with napkins and tablecloths. But after a while, as our restaurants grew, I noticed the laundry service was deteriorating. I told my friend that tablecloths were arriving with patches on them, and deliveries were often late on busy days. As a result, I'd decided to set up our own laundry on the fourth floor.

He was shocked, of course. But then, he was *always* shocked at anything I did. When I'd told him we were only going to serve one item, he'd said, "Your restaurant won't last a year." When I told him about the laundry, he said, "This time, you're really going to lose your shirt. What do *you* know about running a laundry?"

I didn't remind him about the "Simpson's" Dry Cleaners Yale and I once had. But I did say I was starting up a laundry, anyway. He shook his head in sincere sorrow.

My friend and his laundry, I'm sorry to say, are now both gone. He was really a nice man but never understood my way of doing business. How could he? He was an expert and knew what he was doing. *I* didn't have a clue.

In its first year of operation, our fourth-floor laundry saved us $53,000.

Sheer ignorance sometimes beats experience. But you can't succeed if you don't try.

26.

Not everything succeeds, of course, even when you *do* try. The restaurant below Ed's Warehouse is now called Ed's Italian. But when it first opened, serving only roast beef, we called it the Underworld. And to give it something different, I decided to provide entertainment. So I turned it over to a young couple, a twenty-year-old jazz saxophonist named Doug Pringle and his beautiful partner, Kati Hewko.

With 200 seats to fill, they staged avant-garde jazz, poetry readings, interpretive dancing, and homemade Warhol films—and *never* filled the seats. The flop was resounding. I learned a lesson fast:

You don't mix roast beef with Andy Warhol.

27.

The Underworld proved to be hell indeed. So out went Andy, Doug, the lovely Kati, and jazz musicians with names like Sun Ra. And the roast beef stayed.

We served it for dinner from five to ten. After that, up until 1 A.M., we switched the menu to seventy-five-cent corned beef, pastrami, and salami sandwiches, and steins

HOW
TO
BUILD
AN
EMPIRE
ON AN
ORANGE
CRATE

of beer for half a buck. We hoped to lure the after-theatre crowd who were looking for a snack. And that *worked*. Soon we added barbecued ribs and other appetizers, and the room's been busy ever since—especially since it became Ed's Italian Restaurant.

If something doesn't work, you drop it fast and forget it. Then try something new.

28.

Ed's Folly at first also lived up to its name. That's the dining lounge we opened on half of the second floor. It is posh, and plush, with the usual red velvets and Tiffany lampshades, and has intimate little "courting" parlours all along one wall. Each tiny parlour has a curtain in front and, at first, held only a love seat for two. All extremely Edwardian.

The entrance doors are 4,000 pounds of solid brass, ten feet high, which the old Imperial Bank of Commerce had paid $8,000 for when it installed them in its head office at Bay and King in 1928. I bought them from Teperman, the top Toronto wrecker, for $600.

I wanted this room to be "romantic". And because I love ballroom dancing, and the big-band sounds I grew up with, we installed a tiny dance floor and piped in taped music of the thirties' big-band tunes. Personally, I loved it.

But Glenn Miller and his contemporaries proved to be as popular in Ed's Folly as Andy Warhol was in the Underworld. The place was often as quiet as stardust. I'd been wrong again. I thought we'd have to hire a small live group to set a modern mood instead. And at that exact time a man from New Jersey walked into my office. His name was Frank Russo and he said, "Ed, I play four instruments all at the same time—the piano, xylophone, accordian, and drums. And I also sing while I'm playing."

I said, "Frank, I'm in the bargain business. And if I can get five musicians for the price of one, *that's* a bargain. Let's try it."

That was twenty-five years ago. Frank's still in Ed's Folly—all *five* of him.

A good one-man band is cheaper than an orchestra.

29.

So we had our entertainment situation settled. The next problem came from the Liquor Control Board—which in those days insisted every patron *had* to buy food along with a drink. And, since we were officially a dining lounge, I naturally complied with the law. We *did* serve food along with the alcohol.

But the roast beef had gone with the big bands. In keeping with the spirit of Frank's drums and accordian, we'd started serving twenty-five-cent hot-dogs with the drinks. Now I know Ed's Folly is a swanky place, and the idea of serving hot-dogs was ridiculous. *That's* why I did it. Most things I'd done had been based on the ridiculous.

Unfortunately, the Liquor Board thought the idea of

HOW
TO
BUILD
AN
EMPIRE
ON AN
ORANGE
CRATE

serving weinies was ridiculous, too. They said hot-dogs hardly suited the room's posh decor. I heartily agreed. The inspector I dealt with was stymied. There was no *law* against serving hot-dogs. He then said the price was too low. I agreed. Again, the poor man had no idea how I operated. So I asked him what *he* thought a fair price was. He suggested fifty cents.

A *suggestion*, mind you, not an order. And it's smart to follow the Liquor Board's suggestions. So I said, "Okay, fifty cents it is." He was happy. I was happy. We kept selling hot-dogs.

Disaster can often be averted by a simple two-bit saw-off.

30.

So now we had *both* the entertainment and liquor problems settled in Ed's Folly. The final one came from the hot-dogs themselves. Even at their newly inflated price, they were still cheap. *Too* cheap, as it turned out. And the word soon spread. In one of the poshest dining rooms in town, you could buy a hot-dog for half a buck.

Suddenly entire families were converging on the place. Dad would order a single beer—and a few rounds of hot-dogs for the clan. It wasn't exactly what I'd had in mind. Nor did it amuse those intimate couples quietly sipping French wine in a courting parlour.

So, like the roast beef, Andy Warhol, and poor old Glenn Miller, the hot-dogs went too. Instantly followed by the families. They were replaced with a buffet of cheese, olives, pickles, crackers, and salami. Which pleased the dancers, the courting parlour couples, and me.

After all our innovations in entertainment and cuisine, the only one left was Frank Russo.

A good bargain's a bargain. But if you get TOO cheap you'll go broke.

31.

In all our businesses from the very beginning we had a rule of compulsory retirement at sixty-five. The purpose was to provide opportunities for younger employees.

Then suddenly one day I turned sixty-four. And the last thing I looked forward to was being unemployed. It had never dawned on me before.

So I immediately changed the rules and scrapped compulsory retirement. From then on anyone working for me could stay as long as they wanted to, providing they were productive. This has pleased a goodly number of our employees now in their late seventies—including my old pal Yale, to say nothing of me—and some who are even over eighty.

Thus, when I bought the old Lunkenheimer-Morrison Brass Foundry on King Street to put in a new restaurant, the thought about unemployed but still active seniors again cropped up. So I decided to staff it *only* with waiters older than sixty-five.

The idea really excited me. There was still considerable

HOW
TO
BUILD
AN
EMPIRE
ON AN
ORANGE
CRATE

mileage in many senior citizens. The jobs would provide initiative, money, activity, and a chance to mingle with interesting people from around the world. And, while most people think the restaurant's name is simply another example of aging Mirvish egotism, that's why we called it "Old Ed's".

Unfortunately, while the concept was excellent, it didn't work, simply because I *didn't* know that recipients of Old Age Pension, at that time, lost their government cheques if they worked. So most of the oldsters who first considered jobs finally told me, "Thanks for the chance, Ed, but I can't."

Still, there were some older men who hired on anyway, saying they'd rather *earn* their money than receive it in the mail. And besides, the government didn't give tips. Some of them, in their seventies, I'm delighted to say, work for us still.

Although God knows (as Anne and David do) that I'm basically shy, I've always tried to come across as casual: debonair with the public, flippant with the press. It's the flamboyant Crazy Ed persona I've attempted, and too often managed to create. So whenever reporters asked me why Old Ed's wasn't staffed *entirely* by oldsters, I said, "The body count was disastrous. They kept shooting off their skateboards."

It got a laugh. But the truth was that, in order to work, the seniors had to forfeit their pensions.

The mysteries of governments never cease to amaze me. What one hand giveth, the other hand slaps.

32.

When I purchased the building next door to Old Ed's I also inherited a tenant. This was a basement restaurant called Jazzberrys whose owners had invested $250,000 in kitchen facilities and elegant decor. They played live jazz in the evenings. In two years they went broke.

Another management took over. I told them all they had to do was move in and serve good food at fair prices. But they too had dreams of doing something different. I'm stunned at the number of people who open restaurants because of dreams. They may stumble across a quaint café in some small French village and think, "Wouldn't it be great to open a place like this back home?" Well, what's right for Vichy may not be for King Street.

The new people threw out everything from Jazzberrys and installed their own creation for another $250,000. They called their café the French Horn. This one I finally had to take over for arrears in rent.

Dreams alone don't run a business.

33.

So suddenly I have a new restaurant, *and* responsibility. And at that particular moment, I had enough of *both* as it was. So I simply locked up my unwanted inheritance. But, since I didn't want it to look like a white elephant in the block, I placed three large signs in the three front windows, which read: "Ed's Club." "The Most Exclusive

HOW
TO
BUILD
AN
EMPIRE
ON AN
ORANGE
CRATE

Club In The World." "We Have No Members, And You Can't Join!"

Naturally the newspapers called. I told them the club was exactly what it said. *So* completely private, in fact, that I was the only one who belonged. And *that*, you can bet, got some print. But after a few months, the place began to bug me. Here was $250,000 worth of equipment and furnishings just sitting there, and no rent coming in.

Which pushed me into opening yet another place, with a new sign hanging on King: "Most Honourable Ed's Chinese Restaurant. Sechuan & Cantonese Food."

The newspaper boys galloped back to needle me. "So, what happened, Ed? Your exclusive club went bust, huh?"

"On the contrary," I told them. "For a while it was a smashing success. But then after weeks of sitting by myself in this elegant, empty club, I found myself staring in the mirror and saying to myself, 'This is great, but it's lonely at the top.' And finally, I just couldn't stand the pleasure all alone any longer."

The only good restaurant is a packed restaurant.

34.

I'm proud that our restaurant complex has won such recognition as the Excellence in Dining Award from United Airlines, and the Business Executives' Dining Award from New York City. But, besides the quality of our dishes, most customers are curious about statistics. So, in answer to our most-asked questions, each year we serve more than:

- 1,200,000 meals
- 250,000 pounds of potatoes
- 500,000 Yorkshire puddings
- 3 million dinner rolls (from our own third-floor bakery above Ed's Warehouse)
- 500 tons of beef
- 250,000 pounds of fine sifted (*petits pois*) green peas
- 300,000 green salads

And that's not even counting coffees and desserts. So:

Beware of experts who insist it can't be done!

35.

In the entrance of Ed's Warehouse hangs a life-sized photo of an actress named Sabrina who played the Royal Alex decades ago. Her picture is in profile, and Sabrina is amazingly endowed. Dolly Parton could pass as her sister.

One day I was following three junior executives out of the restaurant. When they came to Sabrina they stopped dead in their tracks and for a long moment stared in awe. Finally one of the three men murmured, "Wow, has she ever got a small waist."

I'd never heard such a tribute to Sabrina's charms before. But it taught me this:

There is always a polite way to make a point.

HOW
TO
BUILD
AN
EMPIRE
ON AN
ORANGE
CRATE

36.

Before buying the Royal Alex, I had little interest in theatre — or any of the arts for that matter. I'd never been exposed to them when young and was too busy working as an adult to explore them.

My wife, Anne, and her family, however, had always been passionate about theatre, music, and art. And she's always tried desperately to educate me. Whenever she could she took me along to plays, concerts, even art shows. I'll always remember one cultural event the first year of our marriage.

It was a sweltering, airless summer evening. The thermometer was still stuck above 90° F. The entire day I'd poured sweat in the store and was ready to keel over. All I wanted was to spend the evening in a tub filled with ice cubes. But there was a symphony concert at Varsity Stadium which Anne — even though she'd been working in a steaming office all day — wanted to attend.

So we climbed into a Bloor streetcar jammed with steaming, sticky people to go and hear Beethoven. The bowl of the stadium was even hotter. We were glued to stadium benches as hard as cement. And we sat right behind the *percussion* section. Every note pierced through my skull. It was like I'd been plunged into Dante's Inferno.

But then, when the orchestra boomed into Ludwig's Fifth — "Dah-Dah-Dah . . . *DAHHHH!*" — I nearly shrieked. In those three seconds, our marriage almost screeched to a halt.

But, although at the time I'd have shot Beethoven on sight, Anne's devotion to the arts changed our lives. In retrospect, it's ironic, because, for the past few decades, I've actually *paid* orchestras to perform. And Anne was the one who first exposed me to classical music.

To have the right influences in your life is fortunate. They all pay off in the end.

37.

It was Anne as well who first attempted to interest me in art—although she almost immediately regretted it.

Once in New York she asked me to accompany her to a special showing of some guy's stuff at the Jewish Museum of Art. And man, was it *modern*! The prize exhibit—listed in the thousands—was a pair of king-sized mattresses nailed to the wall. They were split open down the centre with the stuffing and springs all jumping out. Pop Art, they called it.

Everyone was just *raving* about the mattresses, so I studied them for a full ten minutes and still couldn't figure out the catch. At that price, there *had* to be *something* I was missing.

Finally, I gave up and whispered to my wife, "Is *this* art?"

Anne gave me a look and said simply, "Did *you* think of it?"

Well, I learned *that* lesson in a hurry:

If you can't do it yourself, don't knock it.

HOW
TO
BUILD
AN
EMPIRE
ON AN
ORANGE
CRATE

38.

But back in Toronto that stupid mattress kept bugging me for days. If *that's* all it took to be a famous artist, I thought, with a little ingenuity I could do even better myself.

I decided to scour junkyards, find a few odd pieces of machinery, give them clever titles, ship them off to some city like Chicago where nobody knew me, and pay a major art gallery to display the modern sculptures of this brilliant but unknown Toronto businessman. Then I'd wait for the critics to *discover* me.

Our son, David, was just about to open his own art gallery on Markham Street at the time. And I thought how proud he'd be to display the artistic masterpieces of his very *own* father—just as soon as I was *famous*. And how thrilled Anne would be that *I'd* actually *thought* of something creative.

So I secretly collected all this junk. And I got other things from the small Bloor Street plastics factory I owned at the time, which made mouldings. As a test run, I made two sculptures. One was part of a governor off an old machine, which consisted of spheres that swung around on arms. I tempered and polished those orbs to a brilliant metallic blue, then mounted the entire structure on a large green marble base. As a final touch I added a brass name-plate which read:

"Cold Frustration"

By Ed Mirvish

The second work of art was an extremely complicated piece of machinery put together from farm equipment. This I mounted and called, "Chaos".

Both sculptures were magnificent. I was so excited by the final results, I just couldn't wait to create the entire Chicago exhibition. I wanted to show them at once. I considered displaying them in the Royal Alexandra lobby, but Yale Simpson wouldn't let me. His excuse was the lobby was too tiny. But I realized he was right. It was far too easy for some canny art collector to steal them and whip them out the door.

Finally I had the perfect solution. I'd put them in the much larger lobby of the Poor Alex Theatre, which I'd set up as an alternative to the Royal Alex. So there they stood one night when I escorted my wife to an opening. I was bursting to hear the crowd's reaction. But after one glance at my creations, Anne instantly called David, who was in New York arranging his own first show for Toronto, to tell him his father was "ridiculing art". Would he please intercede in having them immediately removed from the public view.

Thus my sole artistic endeavour was shot down stillborn. I've never quite gotten over it. I'm still sure if patrons had been able to see "Chaos" and "Cold Frustration", I'd have sold them. They were certainly cheaper, and easier to display, than a slashed mattress. History is probably littered with equally brilliant ideas that never had the chance to surface. But it *did* teach me something.

HOW
TO
BUILD
AN
EMPIRE
ON AN
ORANGE
CRATE

You may be blessed with amazing creativity, but you're considered a genius only if the rest of the world agrees.

39.

Years ago Yul Brynner was at the Royal Alex starring in a musical called *Odyssey*. It was a subscription show running four weeks. One Wednesday afternoon just after it opened, Yul said his throat felt so raw he might not be able to go on. It was just before the 2 P.M. curtain time, and our matinee performances are usually sold out.

When 1,500 patrons can't see a star of Yul's magnitude, there's trouble. I'd much sooner be on an iceberg in Antarctica at such moments than anywhere near the theatre. But there I was, too late for escape. So I nervously paced the lobby, waiting for the ensuing roar of resentment inside and murmured to the theatre manager, "If Telly Savalas was the understudy I bet Brynner would go on."

Latecomers were still scurrying in. One was a columnist for a major Toronto paper, who overheard me. The following day my appalling *bon mot* appeared in print, and I was mortified—especially since Yul *had* gone on after all.

For me, it's total panic time. Antarctica, by comparison, seemed like paradise. I was terrified that Yul, in understandable fury, would cancel the remainder of the run.

So I instantly sat and wrote a letter. It read:

"Dear Mr. Brynner. My mother always said to me, 'Ed, you got a big mouth. You always talk too much.' My mother was always right. So, Mr. Brynner, when I saw the article with my remark about you in the paper, please believe me, I wanted to kill myself. I can only say that I offer you my apology, and hope you will accept it. It is a great honor to have you play our theatre. Sincerely, Ed Mirvish."

That night I went to his dressing room. Brynner turned and stared at me with those eyes that could paralyse Siam. I knew what was coming, and cringed.

Then he laughed, and shook his head. "Don't kill yourself, Ed."

That was in 1975. Yet even now, with Yul long gone, I still wince to recall my idiocy. But the experience sure taught me what my mother never could:

Always make sure your brain is engaged before putting your mouth in gear.

40.

One star who actually *did* lose her voice *totally* before a show was Debbie Reynolds. She was in a musical called *Irene* at the Royal Alex — being directed by none other than John Gielgud. There was backstage panic seconds before the curtain when Sir John discovered, to his horror, that even the *understudy* wasn't ready.

But the great Shakespearean had learned through the decades that every theatrical crisis could be coped with.

HOW
TO
BUILD
AN
EMPIRE
ON AN
ORANGE
CRATE

"All right," he told Debbie, "you go on *anyway*, and *I'll* stand in the wings and read your words." Absurd as it sounded, there was no other recourse.

So the orchestra blared, the curtains opened, and Debbie tap-danced on stage—across the top of five grand pianos. The house thundered with applause.

But when it came time for Debbie's first solo, Sir John stepped out and raised his hand. "And now ladies and gentlemen," he announced, "Miss Reynolds would be singing these words, if she could."

Then, as the band played, and Debbie mimed, the sonorous tones of the famed British thespian rang out from behind the curtain.

It didn't just sound absurd. It *was*. It was absolute disaster. After the initial howls, the audience fast grew angry. Scores hit the box-office at intermission demanding refunds. They'd come to hear Debbie Reynolds *sing*, not Sir John Gielgud *recite*. And I couldn't blame them. It merely confirmed what I already knew:

No matter how attractive the substitute, you must always give patrons what they PAY for.

Also, **Don't BELIEVE they'll pay to hear Gielgud read the phone book.**

41.

I quickly learned that, with theatre, everyone has different tastes. One man's *Goldilocks* is another man's *Grease*.

So I don't like to stand in the lobby after performances

anymore because, no matter how well a show is received, there's always *someone* who doesn't like it.

But I broke my rule once with *The Gin Game* starring Jessica Tandy and Hume Cronyn. It had been a huge hit on Broadway, and it was an equal smash here on opening night. The audience went wild. Nearly a dozen curtain calls. So I thought it was safe to face the crowd and bask in some unanimous praise for a change.

But, sure enough, after scores of patrons had told me how much they loved it, one little old lady poked her way through the mob and waggled her finger in my face. "Boy, Ed, I tell ya, if the next show's not better, you lost *me* as a subscriber. I came to see some funny show about drinking gin," she snapped. "And all darn night it was just these two old fogies playing cards."

That did it. I haven't been back in the lobby since. I should have *known*.

Roast beef is predictable. Bargains are predictable. Theatre is ALWAYS UNpredictable!.

42.

We once staged a show in Toronto called *It's Never Too Late* —a comedy about pregnancy. With my usual rare flair for offbeat publicity stunts, I decided to admit all pregnant women into the theatre for half price. I considered it a bolt of brilliance.

But when I told the producer of my inspiration, he became enraged. It was, he raved (with accompanying

HOW
TO
BUILD
AN
EMPIRE
ON AN
ORANGE
CRATE

bleeps), not only a *travesty* but an insult to decency, the theatre, the playwright, the cast, the audience, and himself. What's more, he thundered, if I carried out my idiotic scheme he'd yank the show.

"Hey," I said, "so *okay!* It's *your* production. Let's forget it."

(Still, I admit, I was stunned at the man's reaction. Like my two unsold sculptures, another unsung stroke of novelty stifled at birth.)

"Okay, Ed, fine," he finally said. "But *why* would you ever *conceive* of such an insensitive gimmick in the *first* place?"

"It's *obvious*," I told him. "If all the ladies are *pregnant*, the ticket lineups will be *twice as long.*"

I couldn't believe it. He might have known all about shows, but I figured I knew business. And I'd learned from the beginning:

The bigger half of "show business" is business.

43.

After buying and renovating the Old Vic in London, I was inspecting the entire theatre one day just before the grand reopening. And for the first time I noticed the silhouettes on the men's and ladies' washroom doors. The female profile looked exactly like Lilian Baylis, the amazing woman who owned and managed the Old Vic for forty years. The other looked exactly like me.

I was incredibly touched and turned to thank the architect — who, I presumed, had designed the silhouettes.

There was an awkward moment before he informed me that the lady's profile was, in fact, Queen Victoria. And the gent on the Gents' was Prince Leopold of Saxe-Cobourg. What's more, he pointed out with delicate English tact, they'd been on those doors for nearly fifteen decades.

I have no idea how Leo would react to my naïve presumptuousness. But I'm certain Queen Victoria would not be amused.

Still, for what it's worth, I learned another lesson: **It may take a twenty-minute phone call to buy a famous theatre, but it can take centuries to get your mug on the washroom door.**

44.

Television host Adrienne Clarkson once asked me how I'd like to be remembered. What did I want engraved on my tombstone?

She caught me off guard. Unlike W. C. Fields, who said he'd rather be in Philadelphia, I hadn't given it much thought. If I'd been Bridie Murphy I might have suggested, "Here we go *again*." But I'm not.

"Well, like everyone," I said, "and especially as a stage producer, I love long, record-breaking runs. I'd like every show to run forever. No one looks forward to final curtain calls."

HOW
TO
BUILD
AN
EMPIRE
ON AN
ORANGE
CRATE

I also told her I didn't think I'd create any traffic jams in a cemetery. I can understand why mobs queue to get in my store, but I can't imagine anyone lining up to read my epitaph. And I certainly wouldn't want to be stuck in some huge stone mausoleum.

So what I'd like, I said, is to be cremated. And have my ashes sealed in a big hourglass. Then I'd like someone to sit atop a throne on the main floor of Honest Ed's and turn the glass over every hour.

Then all my customers and employees could point at the hourglass and say, "There's good old Ed . . . still running."

If there's any message here, it's this: **To be remembered after I depart, I want to keep my same low profile.**

45.

But of *course* I've thought about death. It's the *end* of existence. And there's nothing more boring.

Just think, after the long scythe swings for me, I couldn't sell a single running shoe, balcony seat, or spare-rib *again*. And with prospects like *that*, I'd be better off dead. So my meditations on the subject are limited.

Living is far more fun to contemplate. In fact, it's infinitely more fun, *period*. But I've given the serious side of life consideration. I've thought about our human tendency to amass possessions. We often say we *own* this or that, when the only thing we own, uniquely, is our mind. It's the only thing no one can take from us. All else is transitory — or far outlasts us.

The Old Vic, for instance, was there ninety-six years before I was born and will stand (I hope) even longer when I'm gone. Some things, like land, last forever. So it's pretty dumb to say they "belong" to us. Of course, tangible assets can be fun to play with for a time, but I learned long ago:

We own nothing! We are all just custodians and caretakers.

46.

In Mirvish Village one summer day I was sitting on a restaurant patio with two other adults and three students, when one of the teenagers suddenly asked what we each considered *the purpose of life*. The ensuing debate grew lively.

As someone whose own student years were brief, I'd felt at that age that life's main purpose was simply to *survive* it. But, compared with the profound philosophies swirling around me, that answer seemed trite. So I listened.

Finally, all three of the students concurred: life's purpose was "happiness" — or at least the pursuit of it.

The elderly lady beside me had said nothing, but then she slowly shook her head. "Happiness *is* good. It's an admirable goal. But, to me, life's main purpose is to be of service."

HOW
TO
BUILD
AN
EMPIRE
ON AN
ORANGE
CRATE

She said nothing more, but her words made an impact.

Without ever encountering Socrates in a classroom, you can still become a sidewalk philosopher.

And, to me, what she said made sense. When anyone says they've enjoyed some show, or even sparerib I've provided, it *pleases* me immeasurably. So?

To be of service IS to be happy. What else brings greater satisfaction?

47.

Our promotions have always been wild. They've been brash and raucous and outrageous. They've *always* gone against the norm. But customers loved them. And happy customers always buy more.

The wackiest—and certainly *longest*—stunt we ever staged was the Marathon Sale and Dance in February 1958. It ran for seventy-two consecutive hours. It was illegal then to stay open past 10 P.M., but I gladly paid the fines; even *those* got us free press publicity.

To kick it off, we put CHUM radio disc jockey Phil Stone in a window of Honest Ed's. Wearing a dangling cap and nightshirt he did his entire midnight-to-dawn show in bed—where a stunning model served him coffee. And all night long, between songs and chatter he'd tell listeners at home, and the sidewalk crowd who'd gathered to gawk, about our next super sale inside.

He also kept them posted on the progress of our

"Wilderness Girl" who was beating her way to our store on a dog sled (led by huskies King and Ucheck) from a village west of Fort William. Her name was Janet Benson, and she trapped with her dad around Lake Saganaga. During her 900-mile trek to Toronto she made the papers daily, and a mob of photographers were waiting when she reached the city limits five days later.

But after we'd fitted her sled with wheels, the police banned her triumphal entry down Yonge Street because the sleigh had no brake. So I drove the Wilderness Girl down to the store instead and, as I'd hoped, the crowds went far wilder than Janet Benson ever was. The stunt gathered more press clippings than any we'd ever done.

Meanwhile, we kept running dozens of spot sales. A washing machine for $1.89, a TV set for $1.98, a genuine mink stole for $1.98, which the Shelburne, Ontario, police chief's wife won. There was also the little boy who bought a pair of nylons for 99 cents, then broke out crying because he thought they were balloons. (I bought them back for $3.) And when we announced diapers at 99 cents a dozen we sold 482 dozen in two hours.

But the in-store draw was the Marathon Dance in which dozens of couples tried to shuffle around for seventy-two hours in a large roped-off section of the store. Thousands of spectators crushed in to see them wobble around in their agony. At the end, a married couple copped the $1,000 first prize. But for three days and nights, it was just like the movie *They Shoot Horses, Don't They?* And just as sickening.

HOW
TO
BUILD
AN
EMPIRE
ON AN
ORANGE
CRATE

Yet, although I slept only four hours a night and couldn't see straight at the end, I *wasn't* sickened by the sales. Despite a fierce blizzard which swept the city during the three-day-and-night marathon, 80,000 customers crammed in to spend $750,000—at a time when most items sold for less than $20, and during the store's slowest month. It was six times more than I'd ever sold in any week of February—and the fines were a mere $200. I learned from this that:

People will come out at any hour, in any weather, to get a real bargain. Especially if you also entertain them.

48.

We held another dance marathon in February 1962. The Twist was the rage then, so we called it a Twistathon, and it ran for forty-eight consecutive hours. And again, it was a giant hit. At one point, police from three separate stations were dispatched to control the mobs *at 4 A.M.* More than 2,000 people were inside the store, and another 1,500 on the sidewalk were trying to crash in. Half were there for the Twistathon, half for the 4 A.M. special: two chickens for thirty-seven cents.

A twenty-four-year-old woman won the $1,000 prize, but it was a lady named Dolly Stark who landed on the front pages. Against the advice of all the doctors (whom we kept on hand for emergencies), she insisted on twisting like a corkscrew nearly till the end. Dolly was pushing 71.

The business result proved:

If an idea works well once, do it again! Sales are never hurt by repetition.

(That was the year we grossed $14 million.)

49.

I've got to mention one final promotion. I decided to hold a big "Pink Elephant Sale". So I rented an elephant, painted it pink, and tied it up in our parking lot behind the store.

In order to insure attention, I also hired an actor to storm up and down the sidewalk out front brandishing a sign which read: "Ed has an elephant out back without any clothes on! If people must wear clothes, animals should too! It is absolutely immoral!"

I considered it one of my better promotions. And, as I'd hoped, it got huge press.

But it got even *more*, quite unintentionally, when the apoplectic Toronto Humane Society tried to haul me into court. It seems that elephants breathe through their pores. And if I didn't de-pink old Jumbo at *once*, they raged, he could easily kick the bucket.

Well, we hosed the big fella down instantly, of course. After all, who wants a dead pink pachyderm in their parking lot?

So the impending demise was averted. But the resultant uproar drew more publicity and crowds *after* Jumbo had been scrubbed than when he was pink. It taught me another lesson:

HOW
TO
BUILD
AN
EMPIRE
ON AN
ORANGE
CRATE

Adverse publicity can often be a bonus—if acted on instantly.

50.

I've always said a free story is worth a thousand ads. But besides the publicity gained from outrageous promotions and stunts, ads are also essential—if they *work*! And for me, the more off the wall an ad has been, the more *effective* it's been. The whole idea is to *jar* the reader.

From the first I felt if I knocked myself *and* the store —which wasn't hard to do from a decor point of view— people would *notice*. If I called *myself* a nut, people would notice. It would grab their attention. So as long as it served a practical purpose, it paid to challenge the trend.

So that's why we wrote those idiotic ads. Like, "HON-EST ED WON'T SPANK HIS KID (But his prices sure hit bottom)". Or "HONEST ED'S A SKUNK (He's dropping "Cents" all over the place)". Or "HONEST ED'S A BABY (But he's never soaked you yet). Or "HONEST ED'S A LAZY LOUT (He won't get his prices up)".

You get the picture. Pretty awful.

But under the ads, we also listed the bargains and quoted the prices.

And although the ads were corny, they were also homey—and they did the three vital things that *every ad should*:

Catch the reader's eye.

Emphasize low prices.

Give the store a unique personality.

51.

Because Honest Ed's has never been a high-class act (except for our prices), it didn't make sense to advertise, for instance, in a newspaper's society or stockmarket sections. And because we've always aimed a sense of humour (no matter how twisted) at our customers, we started placing our ads opposite the comics page. It hadn't been done before, and most other merchants thought us nuts. But business instantly shot up.

The trouble was, as time went on, the position became popular. Recognizing our success, other merchants started vying for the spot. And the newspapers, also recognizing it, raised their rates for the page facing the comics by up to 35 per cent.

We'd led the way. But after that, it was time to buck the pack again. So we started experimenting with different sections—from entertainment to sports to the women's pages. We thought it fun to let our customers try to *find* us. Another nutty Honest Ed game. And amazingly, *that* worked too.

Obviously, the maxim is:

Experiment! If it works, stick with it. If it doesn't, move on!

HOW
TO
BUILD
AN
EMPIRE
ON AN
ORANGE
CRATE

52.

The problem with our dopey ad slogans was that, after a few years, we were drained of new ideas. And so I came up with a *new* one: let our customers dream them up. That's when we started our "Ed-Line Club".

We hung signs around the store asking customers to send us corny new catch lines. If we used them, we'd give the winners ten bucks and an Ed-Line Club membership diploma (which, instead of a Coat of Arms, had a "Coat of Feet") and run their names in the papers under their slogans. They poured in by the hundreds. And some became store classics. Like "HONEST ED'S GOING BALD (But his prices are hair-raising)". And "HONEST ED'S FOR THE BIRDS (His prices are cheep! cheep! cheep!)". Magnificent stuff!

People just loved to see their names in the papers, even in idiotic ads. And it taught me once again:

Anything you do to INVOLVE your customers keeps them involved with YOU!

53.

Honest Ed's wasn't fancy when it opened, and it never has been since. If it works, why change it?

Our own carpenters build our simple shelves and counters. Our clerks still mind their own business, and not yours (unless you ask!). If you want to try on shoes or a sweater, you do it in the aisle; we still don't provide changing rooms. And although we've increased our range of merchandise immeasurably, we still don't sell perishable produce—which I'd had enough of in our family grocery store. And we still don't deliver. If you buy something *big*, you cart it out and lug it home yourself.

Yet our stock in trade is still bargains. Although the Better Business Bureau initially investigated our sales techniques with the scrutiny of Sherlock, it has given its approval to Honest Ed's for decades now, stating: "There is nothing unethical here." Well, I *knew* when I chose the name, I'd be watched. But the message is simple:

If you open a store with crooked floors, you gotta stay straight to survive.

54.

Honest Ed's has always been called "an incredible success story". I must admit it's been *successful*. But I don't understand why people think it's so *incredible*.

Our *basic* business philosophy has always been the same. And to me it's always seemed to be, well . . . so obviously *basic*!

Keep everything simple and keep it cheap to give the buyer *bargains*. That's basically *it*! No hidden miracles!

Still . . . it wasn't always *easy*. The only thing truly "incredible" about the store's success were some of the early hassles I had to face—then hurdle.

Today I suppose I'm considered a part of Toronto's "Establishment"—a status to which I've never intention-

HOW
TO
BUILD
AN
EMPIRE
ON AN
ORANGE
CRATE

ally aspired. When I was starting out four decades ago, Toronto's business Establishment considered Honest Ed's, and me, a pushy pariah. They didn't like my bargains, my ballyhoo, or my brashness. By bucking most of the established business trends I was, in a way, bucking the very Establishment that had *established* them.

But I'd had no training in business administration. I'd had my schooling on the street—where the potential customers were as well. So when I tried something new, it was strictly from instinct. Not because it was proper, but because I thought it would *work!*

Yet it didn't take me long to learn: **If you try to buck an old warhorse, you can often get tossed.**

55.

Take, for instance, the Englander crisis.

One day in 1959, a pharmacist named Norman Englander came to see me. His small neighbourhood drugstore was doing poorly, and he asked if he could set up a pharmacy in Honest Ed's. "Why not?" I told him, "people buy everything *else* in the store."

I offered to lease him seventy-two square feet in a back corner for $6,000 a year, in return for 6 per cent of his gross receipts. "Why not?" said Englander, and he built his counters and ordered drugs. Then he went to the Ontario College of Pharmacy to change his business registration from his old store to mine—and the college's registrar-treasurer, P.T. Moisley, turned him down.

Englander was stunned. "What can I do?" he asked.

"Well," said Moisley, "you could always appeal my ruling to the council."

And when did the council of the college meet? "In three months," said Moisley.

Meanwhile, besides having space sitting empty, Englander got an even worse blow. The wholesale drug companies refused to deal with him. So there we were with no registration and no drugs. We were obviously being straight-armed. And I let the papers know.

The papers got angry, too. "Abject persecution," one columnist called it.

In reply, the secretary-manager of the Canadian Pharmaceutical Association wrote the *Toronto Star*. The reason for the opposition, he explained, all boiled down to ethics. Under the Pharmacy Act, the college was responsible for protecting the public, and "protection isn't compatible with bargain prices in drugs."

Did this mean that the industry was *protecting* sick people by keeping them from buying cheaper drugs?

Does any of this sound *familiar*?

J. C. Turnbull ended his letter to the *Star* with this jibe: "We do not wish to comment on his (Englander's) inability to purchase products for resale, except to say that undoubtedly every businessman, as well as people in all walks of life, have, at some time or other, been faced with the inability to purchase what they wished."

So *there*! The Pharmaceutical Establishment had spoken.

HOW
TO
BUILD
AN
EMPIRE
ON AN
ORANGE
CRATE

We took it to court. And we won.

The Supreme Court of Ontario's Mr. Justice Danis told the college it had no right to refuse to register any qualified pharmacist.

The college was angry. The drug manufacturers were angry. But Norman Englander opened his pharmacy in Honest Ed's. And the *public* was delighted. I learned from that experience more than any other:

If you think you're right, FIGHT!

56.

The Englander case was a milestone in Canada.

Right after it, an irate editorial in the *Canadian Pharmaceutical Journal* warned that the Supreme Court decision "should make all pharmacists wonder whether they are going to control their own profession."

Well, at least they lost their control over *prices*. And our store was the first to make drug costs cheaper.

And Englander *did* discount them—from 5 to 15 per cent. He did it the same way *I* did. No credit, delivery, or mail orders. Customers had to bring written prescriptions to the store to get them filled. Yet within his first year he'd expanded his pharmacy to 500 square feet, and had filled 6,500 prescriptions. Englander was still giving bargains and expanding the drugstore when he was hired away by a pharmaceutical firm, and I took it over as Honest Ed's Pharmacy Inc., continuing to employ the best certified pharmacists.

Meanwhile, we'd beaten the system. And opened the way for other cut-rate drugstores—many of which have proliferated into giant discount chains across the country —where the public, when sick, can buy medicine for less.

It still doesn't mean we'd beaten the Establishment. The Pharmaceutical Manufacturers Association of Canada still boasts one of the nation's most powerful lobbies. Its influence on governments is often amazing.

But then, you already know this. All we did was help drop some drug prices—and still do business.

You don't have to be a philanthropist to take on the big boys. If you win, the public can profit too!

57.

Over the years I've kept facing the big guns—and firing back. I've always fought rules that I thought were wrong, or simply stupid. And I'm proud that some of the victories helped Toronto. Or at least changed some laws I considered stifling.

Like the city's early-closing bylaw when I started in the 1950s. I've always felt any merchant should be able to charge as little as they want and stay open as long as they want to. After all, it's *their* business, *their* labour, and *their* time. And if there aren't any late-night customers, no sane merchant would stay open *anyway*.

Besides every sale, no matter what the hour, helps the city coffers in retail taxes. So why should the law object?

I've felt this strongly ever since I was a kid on Dundas,

HOW
TO
BUILD
AN
EMPIRE
ON AN
ORANGE
CRATE

when (regardless of the law) we often stayed open till 2 A.M.—because we *had* to. Most merchants did. The immigrants in the area liked to shop late, and if you weren't open you'd miss out.

When I opened Honest Ed's the city bylaw stipulated that all retail stores had to stop selling by 7 P.M. I didn't think it made sense. I *opened* late (because customers preferred it), and I wanted to stay open late (because customers preferred that *too*). And who else but the public is a merchant in business *for*?

So again I decided to challenge the system. When I staged the seventy-two-hour Marathon Sale in February 1958, I knew I was breaking the law. The Toronto Police Department wasn't pleased. It sent sixteen officers down to check the store in the middle of the night. When the case went to court, the cops were supposed to be witnesses. The Ontario Retail Merchants Association wasn't pleased. It asked the city to issue an injunction to prevent me from doing it again. The City of Toronto wasn't pleased. It laid four charges against me for breaking the bylaw.

No one (besides the press) was pleased—except the public. The people who paid the salaries of the public servants. The same public servants, conversely, who had sworn to serve the people—to uphold the *public* interest. There is always some irony in a democracy.

Everyone (especially the media) could hardly wait till I went to court—as I had with Englander—to fight the charges. But I *didn't*. In Englander's case, we'd done nothing wrong and were fighting an injustice. In the seventy-two-hour-Marathon case, I'd broken a bylaw, no matter how absurd I considered it. And I'd always sooner challenge a law than break one. From all my years before Judge Mott's bench, courts have never much appealed to me.

So, when a magistrate fined me $50 on each of the four charges, I figured that from the $128,000 we'd pulled in from the Marathon, I could afford it. So I forked over the 200 bucks without a whimper.

But it's sometimes hard to be honest. Neither the City nor the Merchants Association was happy at my capitulation. As bureaucrats, they didn't like to be thwarted. (Still, I'm sure the sixteen individual police officers were secretly delighted to have something more exciting to do at 4 A.M. than check empty stores.)

Yet my initial challenge, I'm glad to say, was the beginning of the end of the early-closing bylaw. The *Globe and Mail* said the City's prosecution of Honest Ed's seemed idiotic. "Why *shouldn't* store owners decide their own hours?" it asked. I argued that stores should be allowed to open at *any* hour, provided they didn't disturb their neighbours *or* exploit labour. Shoppers unanimously agreed. So did hundreds of merchants. And so, at last, did the politicians.

A law was finally passed allowing retail stores to stay open as long as they wanted. Countless shops in Toronto are now open twenty-four hours.

When the people speak, the politicians finally listen.

HOW
TO
BUILD
AN
EMPIRE
ON AN
ORANGE
CRATE

58

Fighting the City for longer hours is one thing; if you lose, you can still sell within the legal time periods.

Fighting to get merchandise is something else; if you lose, you're out of business. And in the early fifties, many manufacturers refused to sell me *anything*.

When Honest Ed's opened, we sold only "distressed merchandise" from fire and bankruptcy sales. All the stuff insurance companies were delighted to sell off cheaply. I bought it in huge batches, often sight unseen, and had to sort it out by hand. Some items were fine, some worthless. It took me hours to grade it.

As business grew I hired others guys to do it. But since my profits were only in pennies to begin with, their wages soon became prohibitive. I finally discovered that fire and bankruptcy sales weren't proving such a big bargain—at least to *me*. That's when I decided to start moving into the familiar name-brand products—and received another shock.

Because I sold *everything* at less than other merchants, the manufacturers of name-brand products didn't even want to *see* me. They advertised nationally—and wanted to maintain the same nation-wide prices. If I sold their stuff cheaper, they said, other merchants would object— or even try to copy me. All of them, especially appliance manufacturers, were adamant: no dice!

And, because I believe merchants should be able to sell a product at *their* price, *not* the supplier's, I got mad. I decided again to fight the Establishment. And this time it was a *big* one—namely, most major manufacturers in North America.

In the end, of course, I got what I wanted. But it took a lot of different ploys and tactics. Some suppliers accepted a compromise. They agreed to sell me goods if I promised to advertise my cheaper prices *only* in my windows—and *not* in the papers where other merchants would spot them.

Some said they wouldn't sell their products to Honest Ed's directly but would quietly agree to deal with some other company which, in turn, would sell to me. The trouble was, I didn't *know* another company to act as a middleman. So I simply *set up* seventeen new purchasing companies on my own.

But still, some manufacturers refused to have anything to do with me. So I started approaching distributors other than my own—and, surprisingly, other distributors started coming to me. The ones I *went* to often agreed to sell me goods in bulk—in return for a piece of the profits, and sometimes other merchants did the same thing too.

The ones that came to *me* were often in a frenzy. They couldn't keep up the sales quotas the manufacturers insisted on, and were in danger of losing their franchises. So I'd take a big load of goods off their hands at cost or a tiny markup. That gave them their quotas, and gave me brand-name merchandise—which I could then sell at bargain prices.

When Forsyth wouldn't sell me any of its men's dress

HOW
TO
BUILD
AN
EMPIRE
ON AN
ORANGE
CRATE

shirts, I sent a bunch of sales clerks to stores across the city. Then, by saying they needed to outfit some school choir or entire orchestra, they bought up thousands of Forsyth shirts—which merchants were delighted to sell at a discount. Back at Honest Ed's, of course, I ran a giant Forsyth shirt sale.

I learned once again:

If you use your brains to buck the system, there's always SOME way to beat it!

59.

Not all manufacturers, however, took my tactical attacks lying down. A few big suppliers pretended to cave in, and agreed to sell me goods—even though they knew I'd sell them for less than their nationally advertised prices.

And so, with a certain smugness, I'd place big orders— then advertise the products at bargain prices. Customers would rush down to buy them, and find the counters empty—since the orders weren't delivered till the sale was *over*. "Oooops, sorry," suppliers would say, "but we had a delay." Some others never delivered at all. ("Oooops, sorry, we lost your order.")

It taught me another lesson that rates right beside the one above:

If you DO beat the system, it will find some way to buck you back!

60.

My battle with the manufacturers proved ironic in the end. For even if I hadn't fought them in their practice of set prices I'd have won out anyway.

At the same time, in Ottawa, the government's anti-trust people had decided that some of the country's biggest manufacturers were guilty of keeping their prices unnecessarily high, and a couple were prosecuted for price-fixing.

And so, in such a climate, many manufacturers had a instant change of heart. Much as they may have abhorred it, if the choice was prison for price-fixing or selling to me . . . *well!* Suddenly a lot of big companies were lining up to do business. "Heyyyyyy, Ed, as long as you pay our wholesale price, we don't *care* what you charge, old buddy. That's entirely *your* business."

When faced with adversity, it's amazing how fast yesterday's foes can become your staunchest pals.

61.

Still, it wasn't just the manufacturers who were finally submitting to our method of underpricing products. Throughout the fifties, other big merchants were watching us too. And they all had to figure that any store grossing $12 million a year by 1960 must be doing something right.

Honest Ed's was the first big store of its style in North America, or anywhere else. And it's still unique. But it

HOW
TO
BUILD
AN
EMPIRE
ON AN
ORANGE
CRATE

wasn't alone for long in featuring bargains. Soon companies like Miracle Mart, Sayvette, and Sentry were opening discount stores across the continent. Tower Mart, which had started in the States, opened a Toronto store in 1960. Soon Kresge's went partly discount, while even Simpson's and Eaton's opened discount warehouses.

This sudden upsurge of discount houses definitely helped sway those suppliers who initially wouldn't touch me. The manufacturers could hardly ignore us all. What the discount chains finally did was make my kind of place respectable—for both suppliers *and* buyers. Now that its got a certain *status*, it only proves what I knew all along:

The only thing shameful about shopping for a bargain is being unable to find one.

62.

In 1961 the federal government passed an amendment to the Combines Investigation Act. It said a manufacturer may withhold merchandise from any retailer who makes a practice out of loss leading.

Naturally, as I was a pioneer loss leader, the press arrived en masse at my door. I told them at the time, and still believe, that it isn't the government's business to set prices. There should be competition, free and open.

All retail merchants should be allowed to determine their own prices based on overhead and operating costs. They must be allowed the freedom to sell as low as possible, and to use their own methods to sell that way.

Besides, any large business that spends millions on advertising, and still charges normal prices, could be considered even *more* of a loss leader—by *losing* huge profits through expensive advertising.

Along with private bedrooms, governments have no business in private business.

63.

Outside of business my only hobby is ballroom dancing. I've been doing it for more than thirty years. And I've even won trophies in Detroit and Chicago.

As a youth I never danced since I didn't have the time. After getting married I didn't dance because I didn't know *how*. But I finally got tired of going to parties and watching my wife dance with every guy in the place but me!

So before David's Bar Mitzvah I decided I'd learn. *That* was one party I wasn't going to miss a whirl around the floor at. I enrolled with Anne for ballroom lessons. And although she dropped out after the second lesson to study jazz and flamenco instead, I've kept right on whirling through foxtrots, tangos, waltzs, quicksteps, *dos boleros*, and *paso dobles* for three decades. Except for the lifts (one of these days I'm really going to *hurt* myself), I figure it's good for me, both physically and mentally.

The trouble is that people keep saying, "Gee Ed, after thirty years you can't dance *yet*."

Finally, after years of ribbing, I've learned to say:

HOW
TO
BUILD
AN
EMPIRE
ON AN
ORANGE
CRATE

"*Listen*, you wouldn't say that if I was studying *violin!*"

In art, everything's relative.

64.

Unless there's a party or première, I still try to be home every night before six—*except* for Tuesdays and Thursdays. That's when I practise my ballroom dancing from 5 to 7 P.M. I never took a lifetime membership with Arthur Murray since I wouldn't give anyone my money to sit on— especially for *that* long. But I still take the lessons. It's not what I'd call a *passion* particularly, but everything I do I *overdo*.

It used to drive my mother to distraction. She worked in the store till she died at eighty-three—from noon till 9 P.M., when a driver took her home. People used to see her in the Ladies Department and say, "Lookit that penny-pinching Ed. He still makes his poor old mom go to work every day." But she loved to be busy. And she loved the store. She didn't think it could exist *without* her.

Besides, it gave her a chance to nab shoplifters. If we talk about passion, that was *hers*. She had eyes like a hawk, and if she saw someone pilfering she'd rush to our store manager, Russell Lazar, and say, "*Where's* Ed?" Once Russell told her I was at my ballroom lesson.

"*See*," she said with a snort, "that's typical! They're stealing his money, and he's *dancing!*"

I learned as a kid that:

Mother knows best.

65.

Russell Lazar started off in Honest Ed's stockroom three decades ago and is now its general manager and head of publicity. Like Yale Simpson, Russell and I have gone through a lot of years together. And it was Russell my mother always went to with complaints about me.

She once came and told me she suspected an ex-convict I'd hired of stealing. I said, "But, Ma, I can't do anything if you only *suspect* him. We must have *proof*!"

So off she darted to Russell's office. "I'll tell you, boy," she said sniffily, "by the time Ed gets proof, he'll be broke and out of business."

That was my mother. But she still kept her eye on the culprit she suspected. And finally we discovered that the man *had* been stealing. My mother, Miss Marple Mirvish, caught him in the act.

It was just another of her many lessons:

When someone tells you something, LISTEN!

66.

People used to steal drugs at the store. They'd often pick up a bottle of pills, unscrew the cap, pour the pills in their pocket, then throw away the bottle. When my mom spotted anyone discarding *any* empty container, she'd scoop it up and come rushing to Russell or me. "*Look*," she'd crow, "*here's* your *proof*!"

When my mother worked at Honest Ed's we had

HOW
TO
BUILD
AN
EMPIRE
ON AN
ORANGE
CRATE

seventeen employees on the security staff. My mom caught more shoplifters than all of them *combined*. This is true.

There was only one problem. At least half of them didn't steal *anything*.

And *I'd* wind up getting sued for false arrest.

But as far as my mother was concerned, *everyone* was guilty until proven *innocent*.

So okay, scratch lesson no. 64. Thank God for the care, concern, devotion, and undivided loyalty, but sometimes,

Mothers don't ALWAYS know best.

67.

When the governors of the Old Vic decided they could no longer manage it, the Charity Commissioners of London gave them permission to sell — *only* if it was offered on the open market, to the highest bidder, by sealed tender.

The commissioners, who by law oversee the affairs of all registered charities, insisted on it. Because, at the time, it seemed that Andrew Lloyd Webber was the only one interested in buying it. He wanted it, as I subsequently learned, for a musical-theatre company which would stage four productions a year, while training new talent in the adjacent annex.

An admirable goal, I agree. And the Old Vic's governors thought so, too. In fact, they *loved* the idea. It gave new purpose to a hallowed institution which was growing tired and outdated. It offered training to young performers. And it promised to succeed since Andrew Lloyd Webber obviously had the talent and sufficient capital. But he refused to consider a lease. He wanted to own it. And the governors had no objection.

But with only one apparent buyer in the running, the Charity Commissioners balked. Back in 1891 the commissioners had released the theatre's freehold with the proviso that it be vested in the Royal Victoria Hall Foundation for "the benefit and enjoyment of the people". They decided it was none of the governors' business what happened to the Old Vic since they existed solely to provide a benefit to London's working classes, *not* to run a theatre.

The commissioners were not concerned with the future use of the building. And the governors, they said, should not be either, since they were selling, after all, their only asset. As Charity Commissioners, they had to be satisfied that the theatre was sold only to the *highest* bidder.

And that's how *we* got into the game. It all looked so simple in the papers. But if it were not for the Charity Commissioners, Andrew Lloyd Webber would be running the Old Vic today. Some of the old governors still wish he *was*.

There are days I wish he was running it, too. Still, it taught me once again:

You can't run a private business by committee.

68.

Right after we bought it, Lloyd Webber offered us £600,000 for the theatre—which was £50,000 *more* than we'd paid.

HOW
TO
BUILD
AN
EMPIRE
ON AN
ORANGE
CRATE

Naturally I was tempted, because that's a lot of money just to re-sign a deed and fly home again, but by then we were committed to restoring and running the Old Vic.

Andrew *then* asked if he could come in as a partner. Looking back we'd undoubtedly have made far more money, with far less problems—considering the mega-millions he's hauled in since. But I told him that I'd never had a partner, other than my family, and never would. And the same went for shareholders and boards of directors. For *me*, at least:

It's far more expedient doing a deal across a desk than around a boardroom table.

69.

After we'd flown to London to deliver the cheque, I was stunned to discover that besides the theatre—we'd also bought its adjacent *Annex*. This five-storey building, almost as large as the Old Vic itself, was opened in 1952 by Queen Elizabeth to house the National Theatre's pro-duction offices. Although the National had meanwhile moved to its own giant three-theatre complex a couple of blocks down Waterloo Road, it was still using the building for such purposes as painting canvas backdrops on its massive "paint frame".

But when I first saw the Annex, I could almost smell the roast beef. It was perfect as another Ed's Warehouse—or perhaps, being London, "Edwin's"?

Yet I knew from long experience that *any* restaurant,

even more than a theatre, must be carefully managed on a daily basis. It needs constant attention. It's not something that can be controlled by long distance. And we live in Toronto!

I knew that if Andrew Lloyd Webber had bought it, the Annex would certainly have been used to train new musical talent. So I made a deal with the National Theatre. They could use it rent free to develop new playwrights, performers, and productions in return for giving us credit in their programs. And that's exactly what the Annex—*sans* roast beef—is now doing.

Besides the Annex, our other surprise since buying the Old Vic has been the success of the area it's in.

From its early days as an industrial slum when added police patrols were needed to control the rabble, and the Waterloo Bridge Company offered theatre-goers free tolls to entice them across the bridge, the district is now so upscale that Old Vic patrons can soon cross the street to Waterloo Station and ride the celebrated Chunnel to France. Even better for us, hundreds of Parisians can cram into the Chunnel, zip beneath the English Channel, and scoot across the street smack into the Old Vic.

Sheer luck often beats man's best-laid plans.

70.

On the subject of luck and location, nothing has been luckier than the Royal Alexandra.

When we bought it, as I've said, the surrounding area

HOW
TO
BUILD
AN
EMPIRE
ON AN
ORANGE
CRATE

was even seedier than the Old Vic's. Warehouses on both sides and a desolate stretch of railway tracks across the street. Yet three decades later, the slum has become a city showcase.

Within the immediate area of the theatre today are Toronto's most famous tourist and architectural attractions. Directly across the street is the magnificent Roy Thomson Hall renowned for symphonies, plus the enormous three-tower Metro Hall, which houses the bulk of city bureaucrats. Behind them are the giant Canadian Broadcasting Corporation Centre, as well as the massive Metro Toronto Convention Centre and adjoining L'Hotel.

But also within stone's throw are two world-renowned, record-breaking constructions: the CN Tower, at 1,1815-feet the world's tallest free-standing structure; and the Skydome holding 52,000 fans beneath its movable roof, the world's largest domed sports stadium. To say nothing of our own 2,600-seat restaurant complex, and the area's newest jewel, the Princess of Wales Theatre.

The district is now without a doubt one of the most exciting *anywhere*. When reporters ask why we ever bought a theatre in such a squalid section of the city, I say I always visualized the area's potential. Of course, to be honest (which I *must* be), I hadn't a clue. I bought it, albeit a gamble, because it was a bargain.

But I've learned that if you're incredibly lucky, as admittedly we *have* been—both on King Street and Waterloo Road:

Bargains can sometimes turn into bonanzas.

71.

One of the major reasons for the Royal Alexandra's success has always been our subscription series—which today has more than 52,000 annual subscribers. So naturally, when we took over the Old Vic, we immediately introduced the system.

Yet again, there was just that one proverbial hitch. London *wasn't* Toronto. Londoners could buy tickets to *fifty-two* different theatres in the West End *alone!* They had *scores* of shows to pick from. If they didn't like those we'd bought for the Old Vic's subscription list, they simply didn't have to see them—regardless of the cheaper prices.

In a nutshell, while we finally got up to 10,000 subscribers once the theatre was restored, the subscription system didn't do nearly as well as we'd hoped. So we *had* to do something different, soon.

It was David's idea to hire the brilliant Jonathan Miller as artistic director. I was personally not aware of his reputation. In fact, I'd never even met a Jonathan before, be it Miller, Price, or Swift. Most Johns I knew were called Jack. But David said, "Just trust me, Dad," so we gave Dr. Miller a three-year contract to produce six shows a year.

Then, almost as soon as the papers were signed, Jonathan gave David *thirty* scripts to choose from. Most were eighteenth-century translations of the Classics. Gulp! I pause here for a moral.

If you haven't a clue what you're getting into, it's smart to have an even smarter son who DOES!

HOW
TO
BUILD
AN
EMPIRE
ON AN
ORANGE
CRATE

72.

David's first real *commercial* involvement in the theatre was around the time we bought the Old Vic. Up till then he'd mostly been involved in his own art and book businesses. Yet he's always been both wise and dutiful. He once told a reporter that most people want to perform for *someone* — whether it's their family, themselves, or a wider audience.

He said that, while growing up, he always knew his mother thought he'd be involved in art, and his father expected him to get into business, and he wanted to respect us both. So, in order not to disappoint either of us, he became an art dealer.

Smart! And also, I must add, most successful.

That's another lesson he taught me:

A clever compromise is often better than a rash decision.

73.

There were major compromises at the Old Vic as well when Dr. Miller took over. But Jonathan and David finally worked out a three-year program. The first Shakespearean productions we staged on our own were the three Henrys —parts I and II of *Henry IV*, and *Henry V*. The second major (and quite daring) undertaking was the complete "War of the Roses", Shakespeare's great historical cycle.

Here were 100 years of history—and it took *almost* as

long to put on. Audiences got twenty-three hours of continuous Shakespeare. They could purchase the entire seven plays with one ticket and see them *all* in one weekend. There was one show Friday evening, three shows Saturday from 10 A.M. to 11 P.M., and another three Sunday in the same time span. And, although it was long, it was powerful theatre. The director, Michael Bogdanov, actually replaced Shakespeare's usual spear-carriers with tanks and machine-guns on the stage.

"The War of the Roses" ran seven weeks at the Old Vic, including a "Survivors' Weekend"—and every single weekend was entirely sold out.

But, besides the Old Vic, these productions went on to Hong Kong, Tokyo, Singapore, Chicago, Connecticut, East and West Berlin, and Holland. Within three years, the English Shakespeare Company took Roses and the Henrys to forty-four cities on four continents, playing to nearly 300,000 people.

With 2,500 props, 600 costumes, and a crew and cast of 50, it was the most ambitious tour ever undertaken by a large, independent British company. What's more, the two productions won five Olivier Awards in 1988 alone, more than any other theatre in England. And most of it was due to Jonathan Miller—as, I'm sure, was the subsequent title of Commander of the British Empire I got from the Queen.

Yet, while both productions were artistically great, commercially they were not. Neither was a moneymaker. One of the main reasons was that Jonathan, preferring

HOW
TO
BUILD
AN
EMPIRE
ON AN
ORANGE
CRATE

skilled yet unknown actors, seldom used stars. And I'd been in the business long enough to know that, even with mediocre shows, stars *fill* seats. I was incredibly proud of the prestige those Shakespearean productions brought, but we are also in the business to make a profit.

So, while it's great to succeed with something daringly different in the theatre, I still believe, as I constantly told Jonathan:

If you ever have the urge to make money, don't fight it. It's not all that bad.

74.

After Dr. Miller left the Old Vic in 1990, we brought in a long-running American production of *Carmen Jones*. It not only made a profit, but gave us the time to plan our new Toronto theatre. From *Carmen Jones*, we then went from the Greek tragedy *Lysistrata* to Somerset Maugham. And now we're back trying something radically different once again—with the updated version of the famous sixties hit *Hair* (the first show to ever show frontal nudity on a legitimate stage).

A quarter of a century ago, we ran it at the Royal Alex for fifty-three solid weeks. Since then, there's been sparse interest in flower children—but the show's music is still great. And *Miss Saigon* has revived new interest in the Vietnam war, which *Hair* was all about. So we brought back Michael Bogdanov, the director who introduced tanks to Shakespeare—in the hopes he could make the old *Hair* stand on end again. Risky, I know, but big extravagant musicals are sprouting up all over.

If you're willing to take a dare, dare BIG!

75.

Mentioning dares, we took a *big* one when we decided to produce *Les Misérables* at the Royal Alex. Not that we thought it wouldn't be a smash (it already *was* a theatrical phenomenon), but because it would seriously disrupt our regular subscription season of seven shows a year.

We knew that many subscribers would feel cheated out of seeing the *other* usual productions. And yet, if we *didn't* stage it, just as many subscribers would complain that we weren't presenting the important shows. It would be awfully nice to please everyone. But in the theatre business, as I've learned, it's impossible to do. Finally, after deciding this musical milestone was simply too good to pass up, we went ahead.

And *Les Miz* became the longest-running hit in Royal Alex history. In its first 1989 engagement it ran for fifteen straight months—and another sixteen months in two subsequent productions. Not only that, but *Les Miz* ran for another twenty-two months in four separate national tours. That's a total of *four-and-a-half years* the show ran in Canada—and was seen by 6 million people.

HOW
TO
BUILD
AN
EMPIRE
ON AN
ORANGE
CRATE

Once again I learned, while you can't please all the people all of the time, to paraphrase my namesake, you can often please a whole lot more:

If you've got a strong gut instinct, GO with it!

76.

My son and wife often criticize me for not getting involved in details. They say I'm too busy running to check all the important things out. In return, I tell them:

If someone's going to cheat me, they're only going to do it ONCE!

77.

While we're on the subject, I must also admit that of all the people I know in the world, I'm the only adult who was raised by his wife and kid.

Because of their education and innate sensitivity, both Anne and David have always been far more culturally inclined than I. But they've taught me much, and still do. Most of my appreciation of the arts today is basically due to them.

But David, as I've said, is also *shrewd*. As an only son, he's always watching me to see how I spend his money.

Even as a kid he'd see me buy an antique for fifty bucks, and he'd say, "Gee, Dad, all that *money!*" Then a few years later I'd see him buy an abstract painting for *five hundred thousand*, and he'd tell me it was a *bargain!*

Not long ago I was in his Markham Street bookstore and saw three Japanese art dealers staring at a giant ten-by-fifty-foot abstract hanging on the wall. It was painted by Frank Stella, the New York artist whom David represented in the sixties in Stella's soon-to-be-super-famous period. I heard one dealer guess it was worth two million dollars.

Another shook his head emphatically. "No, NO. More like *three* million!"

I couldn't believe it. So after David told me he'd commissioned Frank Stella to do the murals in our theatre, I gulped. When he told me the sum, I winced. But I've learned after years of collecting myself:

Whatever the cost, a great work of art only increases in value.

78.

For our first three years at the Old Vic we always bought touring productions, mostly British or American, as we'd generally done for twenty-three years at the Royal Alexandra—for a total of more than 400 shows. But since 1987 we have staged only our own productions in both theatres.

In the eighties we'd become aware that the travelling shows were deteriorating. One reason was the rapidly accelerating costs of production. All the huge hits had suddenly gone from hundreds of thousands of dollars into the millions to produce. And the costs of buying them were fast becoming prohibitive.

There was also a major change in the old "star"

HOW
TO
BUILD
AN
EMPIRE
ON AN
ORANGE
CRATE

system. Except for a handful of box-office names such as Hoffman and Pacino—who, because of their inherent love for the stage, will at times return to Broadway for a fraction of their usual fees—few top stars wanted any longer to commit themselves to long-term contracts on the road. They wanted to remain free for the infinitely more lucrative, and far less demanding, movie offers.

All of it, of course, boiled down to money. And the money was becoming too big. So it's for those reasons we not only quit buying shows, but started producing our own. And it's opened up a whole new world.

When the times change, you not only move with them—you try to precede them.

79.

The one big problem with producing your own shows is that when they're over—unless you tour them—you're left with tons of sets, props, and costumes. Since rental space and moving costs are expensive, the usual custom has always been to scrap them.

But I've always hated to throw anything out—especially if I could sell it. I was in the recycling business before it was invented. Yet theatre props weren't the sort of thing I could sell at our store. And I also had tons of stuff in storerooms over the restaurants that we'd accumulated over the years—ancient European music boxes, wartime jukeboxes, hundreds of stained-glass windows, thousands of statues and vases. So what did I do with it all? Above Ed's Warehouse I opened Ed's Theatre Museum.

It's also known as Ed's Market of the Absurd, Unusual and Ridiculous — but it's the only museum in the world in which *everything* is for sale. And the prices range from 5 cents to $50,000. To build it we used no designers or museum experts. Every display on the floor was put together by a carpenter, three busboys who didn't speak English, and our chef Ricky Marks — who runs it.

We filled it with barber chairs, carousel horses, Peter O'Toole's leather boots from *Uncle Vanya*, Joanne Woodward's rhinestone slippers from *Sweet Bird of Youth*, antique stoves, Oriental vases, jewellery, antique furniture, costumes, three twelve-foot-high wooden cuckoo clocks from Sondheim's *A Little Night Music*, and props from scores of other plays.

But to keep a constant turnover, I decided any items unsold within a certain time would continue to be reduced in price until they were gone. Any items, that is, except the music boxes. Those are the things with the $50,000 price tags. Anyone can play them for a loonie in the slot — but frankly, I'd hate to sell them.

I hope they're still there many years down the road when we finally have to add *Miss Saigon*'s 320 costumes and 250 props to the museum — including her famous 1959 dream Cadillac, sixteen-passenger helicopter, and 800-pound, 18-foot-high statue of Ho Chi Minh.

From the time I was a boy, I discovered the ancient "Waste Not, Want Not" maxim to be true. Just remember

HOW
TO
BUILD
AN
EMPIRE
ON AN
ORANGE
CRATE

what Yale and I did with abandoned electric toasters and Model T frames, for instance. It was only later I learned as well that:

Everything, no matter how small, has a use to SOMEBODY. So never scrap anything you can SELL!

80.

Ed's Theatre Museum wasn't the only new enterprise we started in order to dispose of theatrical furnishings. After renovating the Royal Alex in 1963, we suddenly had a storeroom jammed with things we'd taken from it—from dozens of theatre seats I'd removed to provide more leg-room, to the old Royal Alex marquee itself.

We also still had our old property at Bloor and Brunswick, just east of our store, where Yale had been running a plastics factory since the fifties. So, since part of it was empty, and we had nowhere to put the Royal Alex stuff, we simply moved everything up to the factory—and opened another 150-seat theatre.

We called it the Poor Alex and rented it out for twenty dollars a night to small experimental theatre groups. And the little playhouse did well. In 1966, for instance, six of the twelve plays entered in the Central Ontario Drama League contest were first staged in the Poor Alex.

Three years later, the theatre became even *more* experimental when John Sime's New School took over its management. The New School had started on Markham Street. But when our son, David, decided to expand his art gallery, he moved it into the New School premises, and Sime moved his theatre group into the Poor Alex.

Although we gave up our control of it years ago, the Poor Alex is still bubbling right along. And while every press story you read says the Old Vic was the second theatre we got involved with, it isn't true. The little old Poor Alex was.

As I said above, *everthing* has its use, so don't scrap it. What I learned from this was:

You can even start a theatre from junk.

81.

One thing we *didn't* take up to Bloor from the Royal Alex was a painting. David and I found it in a back room of the theatre that no one had been in for years. It was a study of a nude girl in oil and measured twenty-two-by-sixteen inches. And the signature on it was *Henri Matisse*!

David figured it was worth $35,000 at the time. I kept it in a paper bag and pulled it out to show reporters. It got a lot of press until someone asked, "If the thing is so valuable, where's your proof?" So we sent it off to New York's Matisse Gallery for their evaluation. And the gallery replied that it was only a copy of a Matisse painting they already had.

I asked them to prove that *their* painting wasn't a copy of *ours*. But they seemed to think I was joking.

So! Matisse or not Matisse, that is the question. Still unanswered.

HOW
TO
BUILD
AN
EMPIRE
ON AN
ORANGE
CRATE

At any rate, we have it still—hanging in Ed's Warehouse. People come in just to see it.

Even a signed Matisse copy is worth $35,000 in publicity. (IF, indeed, it IS a copy.)

82.

Once on Robbie Burns birthday I put on a kilt and proclaimed it *Rabbi Burns Day!* I had a bagpiper wail me through Ed's Warehouse and personally handed out free haggis to everyone having lunch. The stunt, as I'd hoped, got reams of free print.

When a bemused reporter asked why I'd done it, I asked *him* if he'd heard of the fame of Scottish plaids and tweeds. Of course, he grinned.

Well, I said,

When it comes to promotion, dress British, but think Yiddish.

83.

The entire King Street area around the Princess of Wales is paved with parking lots. There's parking space for armies of cars. Yet, ironic as it sounds, the first thing we did when constructing the theatre was to put four levels of parking beneath our former parking lot.

There were two reasons. One was that the law required it. The other, of course, was so patrons could take elevators from the underground lots right into the lobby, thus avoiding the usual sidewalk sprints on wet or icy sidewalks.

But once construction was underway, Toronto's other main theatrical producer, Garth Drabinsky, the man who once owned Cineplex Theatres, reminded the city politicians of a bylaw requiring that any *new* theatre must provide *one* parking space for every *five* seats. And our underground lots' 240 spaces were only enough for 1,200 seats. So City Hall insisted we increase our parking space.

Considering the plethora of parking lots all around us, I would have savoured fighting City Hall, as I'd done so often in the past. By pointing out the absurdity of the bylaw in these ecologically minded times, I'm sure I would have won. The old Warhorse began pawing for the ancient smoke of battle.

But cooler heads prevailed. They pointed out that I simply didn't have *time* to fight City Hall. Construction was already under way. We'd set a deadline to finish the theatre, and any delay would waste months. We'd be left with a massive hole in the ground—plus a lot of unemployed labourers. And because they were right, I gave in. Yet to dig a *fifth* level of parking under the theatre would have cost millions more because of the almost impenetrable bedrock.

And so, as a compromise, I bought the old Westinghouse Building across the street—simply because it had a parking lot. I honestly didn't want it. At least four times before I'd refused to buy it, since the *last* thing I needed was another King Street building.

HOW
TO
BUILD
AN
EMPIRE
ON AN
ORANGE
CRATE

Years before its owners had offered it to me for $30 million and I had turned them down. Then, when real estate prices in the city soared, they offered it to me again for *$50 million.* Still no dice. *Then* the economy went bad, and its owners couldn't afford to keep the building up. Their next offers went from $22 million down to $18 million.

Nope, I still didn't want it—*until* I needed a parking lot. And I bought the Westinghouse Building for $10.7 million. Parking crisis: solved!

Buy only when you NEED something. Not just because it's cheap.

84.

I needed the Westinghouse site for its parking space—*not* for the building itself. The entire place was in terrible shape, and we've sunk another $1.5 million into it since just to clean it up. But what, people ask, will I do with the building now?

Well, if Ontario's NDP government continues its plans to allow casinos in the province in return for a piece of the action, I can't think of a better downtown site for one. *Or* . . . I might still build my Odessa Opera House on the lot. The Russians have even reopened their talks about it.

The most recent Russian official came to see me, in fact, *after* the foundations of the Princess of Wales Theatre had been laid. I said it was just a bit late to consider putting an opera house *there.* It didn't faze him a bit. He wanted me to go into another joint venture by opening a canning factory at the North Pole. He said there were tons of arctic char up there. We could make a fortune. I told him even birds with small brains go where it's warm.

Well, he said, still unshaken in his sudden capitalistic zeal, why don't we bring *ivory* out of the North Pole?

I thought he was joking. "*Ivory*?" I said. "It's illegal to sell ivory now, isn't it?"

"Ahhh, that's *elephant* ivory," he said. "The ivory in the North Pole is just buried in the ice. There's tons of it. Come up and I'll show you. All we have to do is dig it out."

He *still* didn't get it. "Listen," I said, "I'm too old now to even buy green bananas."

I may have gotten into both the food and the entertainment business without having a clue about them, I told him, but fish-canning factories and iced ivory were definitely *out*. So now we're back again to discussing the Odessa Opera House.

No matter how rich the rewards might be, you don't leave what you DO know to jump on an ice floe.

85.

I still haven't given up on the opera-house idea. The city certainly needs one. And we could certainly build one for a *fraction* of what any government would spend. The cost of Toronto's projected 2,000-seat Ballet-Opera House had skyrocketed to more than $300 million before the project was aborted by the boys who like casinos.

Our 2,000-seat Princess of Wales Theatre, which took

HOW
TO
BUILD
AN
EMPIRE
ON AN
ORANGE
CRATE

a year to build, is exactly the same size—and cost $23 million to construct. We're talking a difference in price here of over $275 million.

A project using taxpayers' money spends millions alone in hiring firms to find out if they *need* it. Once you bring the experts in, the millions just keep mushrooming. A lesson I learned long ago was:

If you decide to do it, DO it! Avoid consultants at all costs.

86.

One final word on that opera house. I'd far rather see it on King Street than my parking lot. Or *any* parking lot for that matter.

Parking may be the best business in the world. I can't think of a better one. You employ *one* person to simply *sit* there and take in *cash*. You provide no service, no goods, no *nothing*—except expensive *space*! I know all about it, since I've got enough lots of my own—which the city has always insisted I provide. So I know why businessmen love to own them. The lots make *lots* of money! But, much as I like to make a buck, I hate them.

Today, thank God, you can no longer by law put another street-level parking lot on King Street. But I firmly believe *no* parking lot should be allowed in any downtown area, period! They add nothing to any city but congestion, exhaust fumes, pollution, and smog.

Parking is a hugely profitable but ugly business.

87.

The Westinghouse Building when I bought it, as I've mentioned, was a mess. Among the many stray items it housed was furniture from a nursing home. So, besides inheriting a few dozen dining-room chairs, I also got fifty-five wheelchairs. So I had them all lugged over to the museum and put them on sale, cheap! At ninety-nine cents each, the chairs sold briskly, but even at five bucks the wheelchairs just sat there. So we decided to display them one at a time. And beside it we put a sign: "Rumored to be from Raymond Burr's *Ironside*." We didn't lie. I'd spread the rumour myself. And sure enough, the wheelchairs were a runaway hit.

Anyone can advertise. It's the WAY you do it.

88.

The wheelchair ad was a gag, of course. The buyers knew it too, and just went along with it. But, except for the silly slogans we use for the store, I've always been deadly serious about both marketing and advertising. So, just for a moment, I'll be deadly serious.

We live in an age of labels, groupings, combines, and mass identification. The major trend in business today is to enlarge — not so much by internal expansion as by *acquisition*. Often the guiding principle, and initial basis for a company's success, are sacrificed to the concept of *bigness*.

Of course, increased dollar volume is essential to all businesses. What is mass-produced must be mass-sold.

HOW
TO
BUILD
AN
EMPIRE
ON AN
ORANGE
CRATE

Yet many companies seem to sacrifice their basic business philosophy in a helter-skelter rush to expand. It no longer matters what the companies' basic aims are—as long they keep branching out!

Yet ever since we started with Honest Ed's, we have maintained three basic business principles—which we apply as well to all our advertising and promotion. The three guidelines are:

Fulfil a need.

Go against the trend.

Keep it simple.

89.

In our advertising we always consider two distinct objectives of equal importance. One is the *immediate promotion* —designed to sell specific items at specific times. The other is the *overall personality*—designed to create a distinct image (of our store, restaurants, or theatres). While the second may not produce any immediate reaction in increased sales, I learned long ago that:

Creating an individual long-term image has greater value than short-term promotion.

90.

To create store traffic, to increase sales, and to advertise successfully, *every* facet of a business must be considered.

Every department of a modern store reflects the success of the advertising department—and vice versa!

To an outsider, Honest Ed's advertising often seems erratic. Some people still think we're actually out of our minds. They may well be right. But what we do works for us! And basically, *all* that we've really ever done is: dare to be different.

When I started out in business, advertising experts told me that newspaper ads must be laid out in scientifically approved patterns. They said every ad must incorporate such basic psychological rules as point of focus, direction of eye movement, the use of white space relative to body copy, and a whole lot more—which I've forgotten.

Our ads *crammed* the space and had no central focus, and virtually no white space. And the crowds crammed in.

I learned, as I have through all the years since:

Beware of experts who go by the book.

91.

With little formal training, and absolutely *none* in advertising, I was governed only by my gut feeling.

As a merchandiser, I believed in keeping both our operations and our promotions simple. We strove to be both *basic* and *direct*. It wasn't that I was underestimating the intelligence of the buying public; I just didn't *know* any better.

By the time we'd acquired some knowledge of the accepted advertising rules, our success made it unwise to change.

If the formula works, don't switch it!

HOW
TO
BUILD
AN
EMPIRE
ON AN
ORANGE
CRATE

92.

Our aim in advertising has always been communication, not art. Our early ads never carried a single picture of any kind. We ran our ads on the same premise as the store itself: give the public price and value, not frills.

In Honest Ed's formative years, the entire merchandising industry became saturated with stores that offered service to the exclusion of almost everything else. They gave refunds, exchanges, credit, free delivery, atmosphere. It made us even more determined to go against the trend.

So instead of simply supplying little service, we *emphasized* the fact. That's when we ran ads saying: "Don't annoy our help! They have their own problems! Serve *yourself* and save lots of money!"

But we *also* emphasized that, due to the savings generated by limited service, we could pass the difference on to our customers in lower prices. We felt they were entitled to this option. And it didn't take me long to learn:

If you offer a choice between maximum service and minimum price, most shoppers go for the money!

93.

Tremendous demands are made today on everyone's free time by the widely diversifying ad media. Newspapers vs. radio vs. television vs. magazines vs. billboards vs. junk mail vs. telephone solicitations vs. home shopping programs vs. sponsored sports events. Add others ad nauseam.

A smart young radio salesman in my office once demonstrated this fact so dramatically I almost signed him to a contract. He whipped out a thumb-thick leather-bound book, and said, "Tell me, how long do you think it would take you to read this?" Since I've never been a bookworm, I said I didn't know.

"Well, sir," he said, "this book contains one edition of your daily newspaper. With steady reading from cover to cover, it takes about ten hours. And the average person spends thirty minutes daily with their paper."

The kid taught me another vital lesson.

If you don't grab the reader instantly, you lose him!

94.

For years now, I've considered that last lesson vital. With everyone, time's at a premium. And, since the purpose of *any* advertising is to focus attention on your product, you must first *jar* the customer. Then, once you've got their attention, induce them in with a special offer. That's the job of the ad. But even more important:

Once you've got a customer inside, they must be satisfied!

It's the repeat business that counts.

95.

I'll tell you why.

An ad is a legitimate means of focusing attention.

HOW
TO
BUILD
AN
EMPIRE
ON AN
ORANGE
CRATE

Although people sometimes say we use "gimmicks" to sell products, I disagree. To me, a gimmick suggests some trick or deception. And while our ads may often be quirky or flamboyant, they are never tricks or deceptive ruses. We *provide* what we *promote*. There aren't any catches. For I learned long ago that no matter how crazily contrived the promotion, you still can't turn a bad buy into a good one. The end product of all advertising should be *value*.

You can lure people in with an advertisement ONCE. But unless they get good value, they won't be BACK!

96.

While our ads are often brash and outrageous, the reason is mainly to keep us *unique*. We don't like to be lumped with other stores or merchandisers. There is too much tendency today to *group* everything. I've long believed that:

The more people are massed, the more they appreciate individualism when it's offered.

97.

Honest Ed's is often called a discount store. I have always disliked the term. "Bargain" store I'll buy. Not Discount. First of all, scores of businesses and chains use the label, and we don't like to imitate.

But infinitely more important, the entire discount premise to me is inaccurate. It is designed to suggest that a purchasing advantage is given based on some prefixed price. But I've always believed there should be *no* price to discount from.

In a free society, no one is granted the right to fix prices.

98.

Avoiding imitation applies also to our advertising. One year, for instance, we ran a ten-cent sale. A radio station said we should call it "Dimeathon". We flatly disagreed. The label was diametrically opposed to all our advertising convictions. *Everything* seems to be a *"thon"* today—Marathon, Walkathon, Salethon. Again, its suggests grouping, massing, lumping together. And, in our advertising, we've always avoided the *collective*—to aim at the *individual*.

So instead we ran the slogan, "You can have a dime fine time" (having decided that "there is nothing like a dime" might be stretching it), and we played such songs as "Buddy, Can You Spare a Dime?"

Corny? Of course! But the shoppers loved it. Because, as you see, the key words were "*You* can," and "Can *you*."

Appeal to the individual, not the mass!

99.

Because of Honest Ed's single-unit operation and lack of frills, low overhead *can* put our prices below those of other merchandisers.

199

HOW
TO
BUILD
AN
EMPIRE
ON AN
ORANGE
CRATE

But also our philosophy has always been *not* to find out what our competitors charge and then undercut them, but rather to work on as small a markup as possible and still make a profit.

And—since we have no shareholders nor partners to satisfy, no profit picture that must constantly accelerate in order to promote new financing, and no excess rental due to fancy real estate—the small markups *are* possible.

The best motivation is the LOWEST price, not the COMPETITIVE price!

100.

The traffic flow in Honest Ed's, broken down by individual departments, tells us our prices are right. All merchandise is dated. If it *doesn't* turn over rapidly, we check the reason.

We impress all our buyers with the fact that our greatest advertising is the low prices *themselves*. They're recommended by word of mouth from one customer to the next —promotion that can't be surpassed. And it's *free*! Something I learned long ago is that:

People LOVE to brag when they discover a bargain. It gives them a chance to show off their amazing purchasing acumen.

101.

I've discussed price and value. The final thing is fulfilling a *need*. For it isn't the item we wish to *sell* that counts. It's the item the customer *needs*.

Many merchants often lose sight of this. They frequently try to push products—whose only merit are big fat markups!

When the customer's needs don't come first, you come in last.

102.

One of the key factors behind Honest Ed's success, I believe, is the store's unique personality. Looking around at the growing "Discount House" trend, most of them look alike, operate alike, merchandise alike, and advertise alike.

With other merchandisers, most advertising strives for a corporate image that is decorous. They advertise that they're the biggest, the best in their field. But *none* of them seems to be having much *fun*!

We've always taken the opposite approach. We flood the store and façade with bright lights. We pump in lively, foot-tapping music. We strive for an atmosphere of gaiety and light-hearted humour. Instead of bragging, we denigrate ourselves. We say, "Honest Ed's a bum, but his prices are the lowest." We kid *ourselves*, and the customers join in the fun.

For, even before the Romans and Greeks, the community marketplace has always been the greatest show on earth. As soon as Honest Ed's opened, I discovered the obvious:

People spend more money, more quickly, when they're happy!

HOW
TO
BUILD
AN
EMPIRE
ON AN
ORANGE
CRATE

103.

The last point I'll make about merchandising is, to me, by far the greatest factor: *Personnel!*

Financing can always be arranged, space can be acquired, ads can be great, and bargains can boggle, but the indispensable key to an effective operation is always the good employee.

Employees on the floor are in constant contact with the public. They hear customer likes and dislikes. They hear preferences and interests. They can be excellent judges of what can be sold, and what should be promoted. And it's why each of our seventeen buyers is required to spend time on the floor as well—listening to employees and customers both.

And it's primarily because personnel is so vital that I've always felt so strongly about a one-roof operation, as opposed to chaining out. Since employees are in such close touch with the customers, it's essential for me to be in close touch with the employees. And that's far more easily done under one roof. The relationship remains personalized in a world becoming more impersonal.

We've been offered countless opportunities to chain out—to join various prestigious and profitable firms in both Canada and the United States. And we may have made far more money with a vast chain of stores. But I've always refused. I'd have been stuck in my office all day devouring financial figures and reports, and travelling when I wasn't. I'd be removed from the employees. And besides, let's face it, I wouldn't have *fun*.

I know that remaining on Bloor Street, close to our theatres and restaurants, is perhaps a selfish indulgence. But our family has no partners. Who's to say I *shouldn't*? And besides, it's an indulgence I honestly enjoy. Because, being in the bargain business, I found out:

If your employees do all the work, and you take the credit, where can you get a better deal?

104.

When people ask me to have a drink, I tell them I gave up alcohol when I was nine. And basically, it's true. For I drank far more as a kid than I ever have since. That's when my Uncle Harry used to pour me his whiskey-laced milk punch every morning in Colonial Beach. After that, I seriously tapered off.

Except for the rare glass of wine, with a meal among friends, I've never been a drinker. For one reason, I don't much like it. For another, it doesn't much like *me*. I've learned from experience.

Right after I bought the Royal Alex, the late Toronto *Telegram* columnist Frank Tumpane—as famous for his alcoholic intake as for his interviews—asked me to meet him in the Park Plaza Hotel roof bar, his favourite haunt. When the waiter asked for our orders, Frank said, "I'll have the usual." I knew he drank vodka and tonic, so I said, to be cordial, "I'll have the same."

HOW
TO
BUILD
AN
EMPIRE
ON AN
ORANGE
CRATE

This continued for two more rounds. After the third, I was blitzed out of my eyeballs, and Frank was still as sober as post. I *knew* he could drink me under the table, but this seemed ridiculous. "How can you drink so much," I asked, "and not even *show* it?"

"*Drink?*" said Frank, raising his glass. "This is *soda*. My doctor hasn't let me have a drink in *months*."

I should have learned from that, but I didn't. When the Queen Mother invited us to Clarence House for a party, her private secretary, Sir Martin Gilliat, asked what I'd like to drink. I knew the Queen Mum was partial to gin and tonic, so again, to be cordial, that's what I asked for. That's the night, of course, of the famous "Hi, I'm Honest Ed" line. And when I was leaving I headed for the door and nearly walked through a window.

That finally did it. I'd learned at last:

If it's out of your league, don't play in the ballpark.

105.

On the subject of ballparks, I once drove a tractor into the old stadium owned by Jack Kent Cooke at the foot of Spadina. It was in 1953, immediately after the Cuban Revolution, and Castro was being hailed as a hero of democracy.

Thus, when the Havana team arrived to play Toronto, I thought it was a smart, if expensive, publicity move to donate a new Massey-Harris tractor to the freedom-loving cane-field workers of Cuba. Amid much fanfare I wheeled the tractor onto centre field and presented it to the Havana ball players. It not only got the anticipated play in the papers here, but made a front page in Havana. Down there, I was suddenly a hero *myself*. Che Guevara even invited me to Cuba. Naturally, I pasted all the stories and photos on the front of Honest Ed's.

Then! Suddenly Castro announced he was a Communist.

And here I was, not only giving him a tractor but *bragging* about it. I couldn't wait to tear the pictures down.

If you call the shots wrong, back out of it fast.

106.

On my office walls there are caricatures of me done by such famed cartoonists as Bill Keane, Jim Unger, and Mort Walker. There are also signed photos of people ranging from Pierre Trudeau, Princess Diana, the Queen, and Prince Philip to Mr. T.

There is also one of Michael Wilson, who signed it, "As Finance Minister, I learned it all from Honest Ed." Like the Cuban-tractor photo, it's sitting on the floor in a corner.

Never flaunt past failures.

107.

Before we bought the Royal Alex, the rich of the city were often embarrassed to be seen shopping in our store. If,

HOW
TO
BUILD
AN
EMPIRE
ON AN
ORANGE
CRATE

while toting an Honest Ed's bag they bumped into a friend, they'd off-handedly say they'd been shopping for the maid or getting their kid a sleeping bag for camp.

But as soon as we took over the theatre, everything changed overnight. Suddenly secret shoppers could come out of the closet. *Now*, they were *patrons of the arts.*

Everyone loves bargains.

108.

When we first expanded Honest Ed's, we went west to Markham Street. But as business grew, the store had to, *too* —and the only way left was east to Bathurst.

Now it's one thing to buy up small stores and houses for expansion. But on the corner of Bathurst stood a *bank.* The Royal Bank. The bank, in fact, that I *banked* in. And you just don't walk into the manager's office and say, after he's asked if he can help you, "Well, yes. I'd like to *buy* you."

Meanwhile, we did a show with Liberace, that incredible showman who not only "cried all the way to the bank" —but milked the line for years. It was in *our* show he introduced his most famous one-liner: "Remember that bank I used to cry all the way to?" (Pause for keyboard-wide grin). "Well, I *bought* it."

A few months later I phoned him in Las Vegas, and we chatted. He spent five minutes raving about the lake trout Anne had cooked for him. Finally, just before hanging up, I said, "By the way, Lee. You remember the bank next door to our store that I pointed out? Well, I *really* bought it!"

Who needs a gag writer? Life itself is funny enough.

109.

Before *Miss Saigon*'s opening night at the Princess of Wales, we held a week of previews. And, since Mother's Day was during that week, we decided to hold a Mother's Day special. Instead of the regular price of ninety-one dollars a seat, we offered tickets at fifteen and twenty-five bucks for one matinee, and patrons were allowed only up to four each.

The box office opened at 8 A.M. the previous Saturday. But by noon on *Friday*, a lineup had begun. By midnight, there were 500 people in the queue. By 2 A.M., it had doubled. And the crowd soon turned festive. They brought food, drink, music, sleeping bags, and TV sets. They played cards, sang songs, and danced.

I drove down Saturday morning before the box office opened, and the queue ran *around* the block. There were *more than 3,500* people lined up. I went to the back of the line and explained that the theatre only seats *2,000.*

But hardly anyone left the lineup. I couldn't understand it. I asked one guy about halfway down the queue, and he said, "I've been here six hours already, so why leave now? Even if I don't get lucky, it's sure a *helluva* party."

I've seen crowds line up for bargains for decades, but *never* anything like this. The theatre created a longer single

HOW
TO
BUILD
AN
EMPIRE
ON AN
ORANGE
CRATE

lineup than *any* sale at Honest Ed's. Once again to my constant amazement, I learned:

There IS no business like show business.

110.

About those special fifteen- and twenty-five-dollar Mother's Day tickets, by the way, all the expensive seats sold *first*. They *always* do!

When we first bought the Royal Alex, we considered those students and poor people who love the theatre, but couldn't afford the ever-rising prices. So we put aside 300 seats each night at *one dollar* each. I couldn't believe it, but those were always the *last* to sell.

I soon discovered that, regardless of bargains, when it comes to theatre, people want only the best.

Whether a businessmen has buyers in town or a boy takes a girl on a date, they always want to *impress*. And they impress by buying the best seats.

But I also found that, when seats are *too* easy to get, people don't appreciate them as much. So we did two things fast. We cut out the $1 tickets. And we stopped giving out free passes—since we found that those people getting something for *nothing* didn't appreciate them either. Besides, the practice of papering the house degrades both the show and the actors.

So in order to create a shortage of seats in a different way, we devised our *subscription* series—which allows more people to see more shows at prices almost everyone can afford. Today, we have more than 52,000 subscribers who, for a single price, see seven shows a year.

I learned soon after we got into the Royal Alex not only that the best theatre is a *full theatre*, but also:

Theatres draw the most attention when you CAN'T get a seat.

111.

Besides keeping the Royal Alex filled fifty-two weeks a year, one of the things I'm proudest of about the subscription series is that it requires no public money.

While most theatres in the world are subsidized by either governments or charitable foundations, all three of our theatres are run privately, and profitably, without a cent of subsidy.

It's not that I'm *against* all subsidies. I believe that national companies such as ballet, opera, symphony orchestras, and repertory theatres *should* receive financial aid. Personally, I've never had the talent or patience to work with committees—or to cope with the "help" they provide. But I also believe that theatres like ours should be able to show a profit by giving the public the best value we can. For I found long ago with the store, and now the theatres:

If you do YOUR part, the public does THEIRS.

Whether it's safety pins or Shakespeare, if it's GOOD, it will SELL!

HOW
TO
BUILD
AN
EMPIRE
ON AN
ORANGE
CRATE

112

As I've frequently said, I bought the Royal Alex because it was a bargain. I wish I could say I was being altruistic, but it isn't true.

Still, when I heard it would be demolished if it wasn't sold, it annoyed me. Even *I* knew such a beautiful edifice shouldn't be sacrificed for another polluting parking lot. But I had no particular interest in show biz; I thought the building would be a great place to *sell* stuff.

Before we put in a bid, I found that the previous year its *total* stage productions had run only sixteen weeks. (Most of the big road shows were going to the newly built —and subsidized—O'Keefe Centre.) Which meant that the grand old lady of King Street had been *dark* for thirty-six weeks. That sounded bad.

But, after checking the books, I was stunned to discover that the theatre had *still* made a small profit. That sounded *good*. So we bought it—after convincing the executors that an individual businessman could do as well as any board—on the proviso we would run it as a theatre for five years.

I didn't expect we'd make much money. If we did, *fine*. If not, after five years we could do with the building what we wished. Still, in the interim, I thought we should *try* to make it work. I *hated* the thought of any potential money-maker sitting empty.

(Remember when we opened Honest Ed's, I figured if we made enough *one* day a week, we could close for the other six. Then soon we were open all week. Same thing! I hate silent cash registers.)

So we totally renovated the Royal Alex, resolving to keep it open fifty-two weeks a year. To me it was a challenge. Others say it became an obsession. Maybe so. For instance, in 1963 I discovered we had one week with no show booked, so I brought in a variety show headlined by Billy Daniels. But Billy certainly didn't work his *Old Black Magic* in *our* theatre. His fans had all moved to Arizona.

That was a week we *should* have kept the Royal Alex dark. And it didn't take me long to learn a major lesson:

As long as you keep a theatre locked, you KNOW how much it costs every week. Once you open the doors and put on a show it can drive you into bankruptcy.

113.

Fortunately, after our five-year period was up, we were not only breaking even but even making a small profit. By then, there was *no* way I'd give the Royal Alex up. From a business standpoint, it was proving its potential.

But far more important, I had developed an affection for theatre. I had found that among all the arts it is the most unique—because it's performed by living people in front of a live audience. There is a wonder to theatre because it is subject both to human frailty and to human genius. No two performances of any show are ever exactly the same. It is vibrant because it is *alive*.

An intimate rapport spans the spotlights between

HOW
TO
BUILD
AN
EMPIRE
ON AN
ORANGE
CRATE

audience and actor which no motion picture or TV screen can achieve. There is also a grandeur of *setting*. Theatre is an *occasion*. We go to the theatre as something *special*, as something that gives us an insight into ourselves, our society, our morality and our times. It takes us out of our daily grind for an evening of shared grandeur.

Theatre is like a love affair. Utterly frustrating when it fails, but sheer magic when it flourishes.

114.

I'm frequently asked to address various organizations. Mostly I turn down these invitations because I'm too busy. But sometimes, when I *do* accept, I find certain members take themselves, and *me*, far more seriously than I do. So I always try to keep it light.

For instance, I was once the guest speaker at a Royal Commonwealth Society luncheon. But my introduction was so effusive, so embarrassingly *gushing*, that when I finally got to the podium all I could say was, "Thank you, Mr. President. But if I was just *half* as good as all that, I'd convert to Catholicism and let the Pope decree me a saint."

Then, to *further* keep things in perspective, I said: "I would like to remind you that this luncheon cost you $25. Of that, $24.75 is for the food. The other 25 cents is for my talk."

Still, I said I'd accepted because of a lesson I'd learned — which, for years, has kept me from going broke:

Always work cheap. That way you're never unemployed.

OR
121
LESSONS
I
NEVER
LEARNED
IN
SCHOOL

115.

On my birthdays I throw a party in Mirvish Village. It's wide open to the public, and usually about 25,000 people show up.

In the store in the morning I stand at the door and give presents to the customers, like cases of Coke and watches. Around noon in my second-floor office, a couple of hundred personal friends show up for drinks and a buffet. Meanwhile, out on Markham Street, clowns and jugglers roam through the crowd, and tables are loaded with free food ranging from pizzas to pasta dishes. In the early afternoon, I go to an outdoor stage and cut the cake.

On my seventy-seventh birthday, opera star Maureen Forrester sang "The Man We Love" with special lyrics. Then, after I'd thanked our friends, neighbours, and customers for coming, Mayor Art Eggleton made a speech. It was very complimentary—and I have an absolutely unlimited capacity for accepting accolades. It was a totally delightful day.

Later that night, at home Anne said to me, "You know, Ed, I think you're starting to mature."

I was hurt.

"I hope not," I told her. "I'd hate to lose my childlike qualities."

HOW
TO
BUILD
AN
EMPIRE
ON AN
ORANGE
CRATE

It may sound appropriately juvenile to say this, but it's one of the major lessons life has taught me:

You don't grow old if you PERSIST in staying young.

116.

People often say to me, "Ed, you're nudging eighty. You've been working nearly seventy years. You've made more than enough to be comfortable with. Why don't you *retire*?"

Good question! The only problem is that people have been asking it for *decades*.

But I always give them reasons. I tell them I first dreamed of retirement (whatever it is) at fifteen, on my way to buy groceries for our family store. I was pushing my bike up a hill near the Humber River and saw some guys dangling their feet in the water. And I thought, how about that? If I could ever earn enough to do *that* all day, it would be nirvana.

That was my dream of retirement.

Yet for years I kept on pushing my bike up the Humber hill. Not to *amass* money, because I didn't know you could *do* that. Nor was it even to *make* money. It was simply to make enough for *food*. I was hungry and wanted to eat regularly.

As a kid I never worked for the *joy* of it. I didn't know there could be any pleasure *in* it. And I'd never even *heard* of the merits of the "work ethic". Quite simply the whole family worked to *survive*. We knew if we didn't we'd be even worse off than we were.

Even though it sounds maudlin, I've *yet* to dangle my toes in the Humber. For even as a child I learned:

If you wait to be GIVEN something in life, you're in for a lifelong wait.

117.

As a young man I always said the biggest thrill in life was to make money. And I did. But then I discovered that an even bigger thrill was a *challenge*! I've never really believed in the impossible. I found it a thrill to challenge new endeavours—and *succeed* at them. There's an enormous excitement in building something new.

Of course, I got involved in businesses that people with training or experience would have shunned—because they'd know the dangers involved. I got into *everything* because of sheer ignorance.

Yet still, I repeat, I never *planned* to get into new things —until the opportunities presented themselves. I never intended to get into theatres or restaurants. They all just *evolved*. Yet *everything* I've gotten into started small and *then* developed.

I've done things as a challenge to make them work, and hope others can benefit by them. At the same time, I've always tried to do what satisfies *me* and hope others get the same satisfaction.

Still, it's only after a project reaches its capacity achievement that I move on to something else. As long as

HOW
TO
BUILD
AN
EMPIRE
ON AN
ORANGE
CRATE

I'm healthy I'm constantly looking for new projects. New *adventures!*

If I went bust tomorrow, I'd start a new store.

118.

When you're young and starting off, you look for acquisitions. So you start collecting things . . . then more things. And after a while, unless you're *using* them, you suddenly realize that you're only *collecting* stuff. We all know we can't take it with us—*wherever* we're going. It was when I stopped to think of this that I realized we are only *custodians* for a while. And yet, as caretakers, it's incumbent on us to look *after* these things. You don't, for instance, let magnificent old theatres fade away.

Still, I learned as a kid,

To do anything worthwhile, you have to make the money first.

119.

Ahhh, money! I guess it's all tied into the same reasons I don't retire. Because it not only enables you to *build and buy* worthwhile things, it also affords you the time to have *fun.*

And, in my case, having fun is what I do every day. I rise early every morning, seven days a week, to be in my office by eight. I answer my mail (by jotting notes on the backs of envelopes, then handing them over to be typed), return my phone messages, discuss store business with Russell Lazar, then wander through the aisles to talk with customers.

At noon, I drive down to King Street and go over business with my old pal Yale, who—after running the Royal Alex for years—is still in control of all the restaurants. After lunch, either private or business, I go to the Royal Alex and the Princess of Wales, have meetings with David or the various managers to discuss different projects both in London and Toronto. Then I usually stop at the cleaner's or grocery store on the way home. Unless, of course, I go ballroom dancing.

Honest Ed's, the restaurants, the theatres, Mirvish Village. Four different environments. And in every one I meet fascinating people from around the world—customers, actors, friends. Every day is different, every day challenging. It's exciting.

I mentioned before those kids on Markham Street years ago discussing "happiness". Since then I've learned a great lesson.

Happiness is being able to do WHAT you want to do WHEN you want to do it.

120.

Well, okay, you say, it doesn't sound as if I work very hard at all these days. And it's true. David and the other chaps do most of the work. I'm mostly having fun.

But still, I've worked hard for most of my life *not* to

HOW
TO
BUILD
AN
EMPIRE
ON AN
ORANGE
CRATE

have a job at all. And now I've found that not having a job is the most *full-time* job of all. Every hour of my day is full.

So I really wouldn't *know* what to do if I retired. I've come to believe:

There's no difference between working and loafing if what you do is fun.

121.

————

I think at *my* age, society *expects* you to retire. People think if you've passed a proverbial milestone, you're over the proverbial hill. They expect you to go off to some green valley, or golf course, and rest. Well, I don't know too many valleys, and I can't play golf. If I wanted a great *no-risk* business to retire on, I'd invest in a few more parking lots.

I observed long ago that one of the strongest needs in most human beings is *change*. People need change to keep life from being dull. They take expensive holidays away from their everyday jobs because, they say, they need a *rest*. Then they burn up more energy in two weeks than they do the other fifty.

But I've been blessed. I don't need a change, or even want one. I enjoy too much what I do *every* day.

So *when* is it time to retire? I haven't a clue. But I do know *this*. Of all the lessons I've learned in life, it's one of the most vital. Whatever in life it is you do:

Every morning it's important to have a REASON for getting up.

EPILOGUE

I've had a reason for getting up every morning for nearly eighty years.

My wife, my son, my parents, my siblings, my colleagues, my employees, customers, and friends. The struggles, the successes. The challenges, the victories. The smell of both the roast beef and the greasepaint.

I supply food, entertainment, and merchandise to the masses, and make it easy for them to enjoy the services we supply. That's been my goal, and it's also been my pleasure. And my only request to the reader is this: if you've learned anything from this book at all, please don't open a business next door and cut prices.

I've been extremely lucky all my life. If it's fate, I thank it. For my road has been not only rewarding but, to me, quite amazing.

It's taken me from Colonial Beach to Buckingham Palace.

ACKNOWLEDGEMENTS

To my thousands of employees, customers, friends, and business associates who made most of these events happen.

To my wife, Anne, for her meticulous review of the final draft, and for helping to prevent me over the years from doing things that were totally irrational. Thanks, Annie, for keeping me in line.

To my son, David, and his family who have had to endure and understand many of my involvements which I often didn't even understand myself.

To my general manager, Russell Lazar, for his constant assistance in gathering material for this book.

To my publisher, Anna Porter, to whom I said, "I've forgotten a lot over seventy-nine years." But after she mentioned money, I suddenly remembered everything.

And to my friend Paul King, the writer I make laugh, for his invaluable help in penning and polishing this story.

220